IRON CONDOR DECODED

Strategic Earnings through Options

Hayden Van Der Post

Reactive Publishing

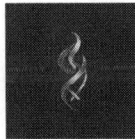

CONTENTS

PREFACE

Welcome to "Iron Condor Decoded: Strategic Earnings through Options." This book was conceptualized with a clear objective: to delve deeper into options trading by unwrapping one of its most strategies – the Iron Condor. It is designed for traders and investment professionals who are no strangers to the basics of options trading but yearn to elevate their knowledge and application in this sophisticated domain.

Having navigated through the vast sea of financial literature, you may have encountered the concept of the Iron Condor strategy in passing or even applied it in its most rudimentary form. This strategy, celebrated for its potential to generate returns while managing risk, stands as a beacon for those seeking to refine their trading skills. "Iron Condor Decoded" is intended for individuals who have previously engaged with options trading literature, possibly even having read some of the best sellers on the subject, and are now searching for a resource that bridges the gap between theory and advanced application.

This book takes a step further from the conventional approach by dissecting the Iron Condor strategy through a lens that combines theoretical depth with practical insights. Each chapter builds upon the last, transitioning smoothly from the foundational concepts of options trading to the details of the Iron Condor strategy. Our discourse will not only encompass the mechanics of setting up and adjusting Iron Condors but will also navigate through the less charted waters of psychological preparedness, risk management, and market analysis.

Targeted at professionals eager to sharpen their trading acumen, "Iron Condor Decoded" offers a blend of practical examples, matched with advanced theoretical discussions. These elements are designed to resonate with readers seeking to not just understand but master the application of Iron Condors in dynamic market conditions. Moreover, the practical examples cited in this book are drawn from real-life scenarios, providing you with a toolkit that is both relevant and adaptable to your trading endeavors.

As you embark on this journey with us, remember that "Iron Condor Decoded" is more than just a manual or a guide. It is a companion in your quest for strategic earnings through options trading. We aim not only to enhance your understanding but to also inspire innovation in how you apply the Iron Condor strategy in pursuit of your financial goals.

Thank you for choosing to explore the nuanced world of options trading with us. Whether your aim is to diversify your investment portfolio, manage risk more effectively, or simply quench your thirst for advanced trading knowledge, "Iron Condor Decoded" is here to guide you through each step of the way. Together, let's unlock the secrets to strategic earnings and elevate your trading journey to new heights.

INTRODUCTION

The Iron Condor is a sophisticated options trading strategy designed for traders who seek to profit from a stock or market index remaining within a specific price range over a certain period. This strategy is particularly favored for its ability to generate income in a neutral or sideways market.

1. Composition

The Iron Condor consists of four options contracts on the same underlying asset with the same expiration date but different strike prices. It combines a bull put spread (selling a put option at a higher strike price and buying a put option at a lower strike price) and a bear call spread (selling a call option at a lower strike price and buying a call option at a higher strike price).

2. Objective

The primary goal of an Iron Condor is to collect premium income from the options that expire worthless, provided the underlying asset's price remains within the range of the middle strike prices. Traders utilize this strategy when they anticipate low volatility in the market and expect the underlying asset to trade within a predictable range.

3. Profit and Risk

The maximum profit potential of an Iron Condor is limited to the net premium received for selling the options spreads. This occurs when the underlying asset's price stays between the inner strike prices of the sold options until expiration. Conversely, the maximum risk is also limited and occurs if the price of the underlying asset moves beyond the outer strike prices. The risk is the difference between the strikes of either the call spread or the put spread (whichever is greater), minus the net premium received.

4. Adjustments and Management

Traders may need to adjust their Iron Condor positions if the underlying asset's price moves against them significantly. Adjustments can include rolling the threatened side of the position further out in time or price, potentially reducing the maximum risk or extending the breakeven points. Effective risk management is crucial, and traders often set exit strategies at the onset to minimize potential losses.

5. Considerations

Executing an Iron Condor requires a good understanding of options trading, including how to read the market's volatility. Traders must also consider transaction costs, as four options contracts are involved in each trade, which can eat into the profitability of the strategy.

6. Suitable Conditions

The Iron Condor strategy thrives in stable markets with low to moderate volatility. It's less about predicting market direction and more about betting on the stability of the market over the duration of the options contracts.

The Iron Condor is a nuanced strategy that offers traders a way to capitalize on market stability. While it comes with a defined risk and reward, its success hinges on proper execution, vigilant monitoring, and timely adjustments. Ideal for experienced traders, this strategy underscores the importance of understanding market conditions and options mechanics.

FIG 1: IRON CONDOR RISK PROFILE.

Iron Condor Example

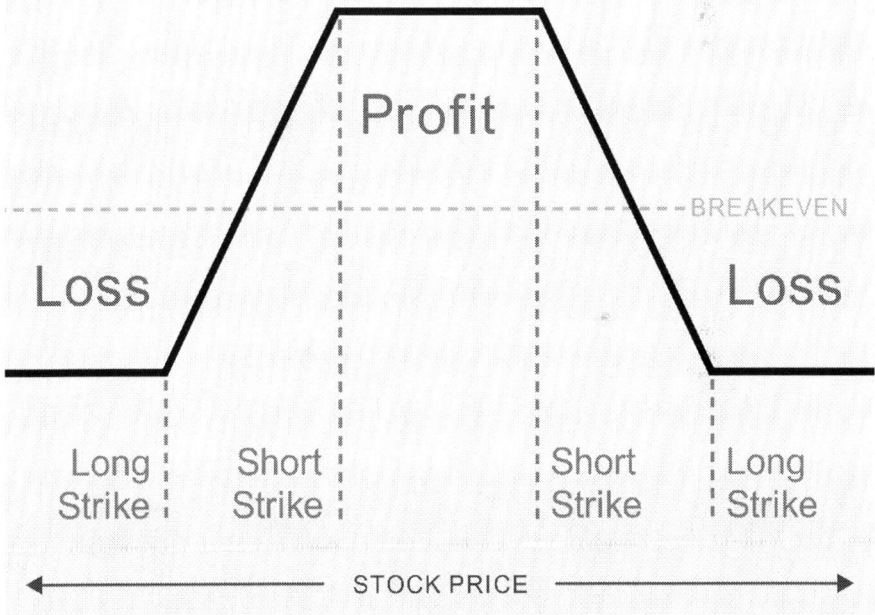

Iron Condor

Financial Mathematics

The mathematics behind the Iron Condor options trading strategy is centered on calculating the potential profit, potential loss, and break-even points, based on the premiums received and paid for the options involved. Here's a detailed explanation of the calculations:

1. Components of an Iron Condor

- Sell 1 call option with a lower strike price (Call A)
- Buy 1 call option with a higher strike price (Call B)
- Sell 1 put option with a higher strike price (Put A)
- Buy 1 put option with a lower strike price (Put B)

The sold options (Call A and Put A) are closer to the current price of the underlying asset, while the bought options (Call B and Put B) are further out. The options are chosen such that Call A and Put A have higher premiums than Call B and Put B, allowing the trader to collect a net premium upfront.

2. Maximum Profit

The maximum profit for an Iron Condor is the net premium received from setting up the strategy. This is calculated as follows:

Maximum Profit=Premium received from selling Call A and Put A-Premium paid for buying Call B and Put BMaximum Profit=Premium received from selling Call A and Put A -Premium paid for buying Call B and Put B

3. Maximum Loss

The maximum loss occurs if the price of the underlying asset moves beyond the strike prices of the bought options (Call B or Put B). It is calculated as the difference between the strike prices of the options in either the call spread or the put spread (whichever is wider) minus the net premium received. Assuming the call and put spreads are of equal width, the formula is:

Maximum Loss=(Strike Price of Call B-Strike Price of Call A)×100-Net Premium ReceivedMaximum Loss=(Strike Price of Call B-Strike Price of Call A)×100-Net Premium Received

or equivalently for the puts:

Maximum Loss=(Strike Price of Put A-Strike Price of Put B)×100-Net Premium ReceivedMaximum Loss=(Strike Price of Put A-Strike Price of Put B)×100-Net Premium Received

4. Break-even Points

There are two break-even points for an Iron Condor, one for the upper limit and one for the lower limit of the underlying asset's price at expiration. They are calculated as follows:

- **Upper Break-even Point**: Strike Price of Call A+Net Premium Received

- **Lower Break-even Point**: Strike Price of Put A-Net Premium Received

5. Considerations

The calculations assume that each option contract controls 100 shares of the underlying asset, which is standard. The net premium received is the critical component that determines both the maximum profit and the cushion against losses. Transaction costs are not included in these calculations but can affect the overall profitability of the strategy.

Practical Example:

Let's say a trader notices a stock priced at $112 and decides to construct an iron condor by selling a put spread (110-105) and a call spread (115-120), securing a credit of $2.59. This strategy implies the trader receives $259 for every contract pair, considering each contract typically covers 100 shares, with a maximum risk of $5 minus the $2.59 credit, equating to a risk of $2.41 per contract (or $241 for a standard contract) before accounting for transaction costs.

If the stock price remains above $110 and below $115 by the expiration date, then both option spreads are likely to expire without value, allowing the trader to retain the initial $2.59

credit per contract as profit, minus any transaction fees.

However, it's important to remember that once a short option position is initiated, the option buyer has the right to exercise their option at any point up until expiration, regardless of how deep in the money the option is. For those needing a recap on how option expiration works, it's crucial to grasp these fundamentals.

Interestingly, even though the trader engages in both a put and a call spread, the maximum financial risk does not increase beyond $241 per spread. But, the strategy does broaden the range of potential market movements that could result in a loss. For example, with just the put spread, as long as the stock's price stays above $110 until expiration, and barring early assignment, the position could expire worthless. The stock price could surge beyond this level—whether it's $115, $125, or even $200— without affecting the outcome.

On the flip side, had the trader only sold the call spread, the stock could decline indefinitely; provided it stays below $115 by expiration, the call spread would similarly expire worthless.

The effectiveness of the iron condor hinges on the stock's price remaining within a certain range. This makes the choice of strike prices critical to the strategy's success. Consider the example given, with 48 days left until expiration. A risk graph could depict a "one standard deviation" range in a lighter shade, based on the current implied volatility. This suggests that, according to the pricing of options at the time, there's roughly a 68% chance the stock will stay within this range until expiration. But remember, these are probabilities, not certainties; market outcomes can always vary.

Lastly, carrying options positions to expiration comes with its own set of risks. Unexpected exercises or assignments can happen, or anticipated events might not occur as expected.

CHAPTER 1:
INTRODUCTION TO
OPTIONS TRADING

O ptions trading, with its roots stretching back to ancient civilizations, has evolved dramatically, mirroring the complexity and dynamism of modern financial markets. Initially simple agreements, options have metamorphosed into sophisticated instruments traded on global platforms. This evolution reflects the adaptation of financial markets to the ever-changing landscape of economic needs and technological advancements.

An option is fundamentally a contract granting the buyer the right, but not the obligation, to buy (call option) or sell (put option) an underlying asset at a specified price (strike price) within a fixed period or on a specific date (expiration date). The seller of the option, in turn, assumes the obligation to fulfill the contract if the buyer elects to exercise the option.

Call options embody the anticipation of a rising market, enabling buyers to clinch assets at prices below future market values. Conversely, put options cater to bearish sentiments, allowing sellers to hedge against or profit from declining asset prices. This dichotomy furnishes traders with tools to navigate both ascents and troughs in the market, crafting strategies tailored to their market outlook and risk tolerance.

The option premium, the price paid by the buyer to the seller, encapsulates the value of choice. This price is sculpted by various factors, including the underlying asset's current price, strike price, time to expiration, volatility, and even the risk-free interest rate. The premium represents the cost of the potential the option offers, a fundamental concept that traders must grasp to navigate the options market effectively.

Options trading opens a spectrum of strategic possibilities, from simple protective measures to complex speculative plays. It allows traders to leverage their capital, manage risk, and exploit market volatility. Unlike direct stock trading, options offer greater flexibility, enabling strategies that can profit from market stasis, direction, and even the lack of movement, with known and limited risk.

At the intersection of risk and reward, options trading unfolds a strategic canvas, inviting traders to paint their market visions with precision and creativity. It is here, in the crafting of strategies from the simple to the Byzantine, that the true art of options trading is revealed. Each strategy, a unique blend of risk, reward, and market hypothesis, challenges traders to align their market outlook with their risk appetite.

As we chart the course deeper into options trading, remember, the journey is both a test and a testament to the trader's acumen, discipline, and creativity. Understanding the foundational elements of options trading is akin to setting the sails for a voyage across the tumultuous yet rewarding seas of financial markets. With the compass of knowledge and the map of strategies, traders are poised to navigate options with confidence and acuity.

In the chapters that follow, we will delve into the mechanics, strategies, and nuances of options trading with a focus on the iron condor strategy, decoding its complexities, and demystifying its application. This journey, while challenging, promises the reward of mastery over one of the most versatile instruments in the financial markets. Welcome to the odyssey of options trading.

Understanding Call and Put Options

A call option grants the holder the prerogative to purchase an underlying asset at a predetermined price—the strike price —before the contract expires. This instrument is a bet on the asset's price climbing above the strike price within the option's life, offering an opportunity to capture profit from the asset's potential appreciation without committing a significant capital outlay upfront. When traders speculate on bullish market conditions or seek to hedge other positions within their portfolio, call options become a critical tool in their arsenal.

The intrinsic value of a call option surges as the market price of the underlying asset ascends above the strike price, rendering the option increasingly profitable. However, should the market price not reach the strike price by the expiration date, the option expires worthless, and the trader's loss is confined to the premium paid for the option.

Conversely, a put option embodies the right to sell the underlying asset at the strike price until the option's expiration. This mechanism is particularly appealing in bearish market scenarios, allowing traders to profit from anticipated declines in asset prices or to employ as a protective measure against potential drops in the value of assets they hold.

The valuation of put options inversely correlates with the asset's market price. As the underlying asset's price diminishes below the strike price, the put option's value escalates, offering a hedge against downturns or a speculative pathway to profit from market pessimism. Yet, if the asset's price remains above the strike price at expiration, the put option becomes worthless, limiting the investor's loss to the initially paid premium.

The strategic allure of call and put options lies in their versatility. Traders equipped with a nuanced understanding of these instruments can craft a multitude of strategies that range from straightforward bets on market direction to complex combinations that exploit nuanced views on volatility, time decay, or even lack of movement within the market.

For example, by simultaneously holding a call and a put option on the same asset with the same expiration but different strike prices, traders can create a position that profits from volatility regardless of the market's direction. This strategy, known as a straddle, exemplifies how call and put options can be synergized to capitalize on market dynamics.

Within iron condor strategies, call and put options are the building blocks. An iron condor is constructed by combining a bear call spread with a bull put spread, effectively selling out-of-the-money call and put options while protecting these positions with further out-of-the-money bought call and put options. This strategy bets on the underlying asset's price finishing between the two strikes at expiration, capturing premium while limiting risk.

Understanding call and put options is akin to mastering the alphabet before composing poetry. These fundamental instruments open up a world of strategic depth and flexibility, allowing traders to express nuanced market views with precision. As traders progress through the odyssey of options trading, the knowledge and application of call and put options serve as critical waypoints in their journey towards mastering more sophisticated strategies, including the revered iron condor.

In sum, the comprehension of call and put options is not merely an academic exercise but a practical necessity for any trader aspiring to navigate the options market with confidence and finesse. As we delve deeper into specific strategies and their applications in subsequent sections, the foundational knowledge of calls and puts will illuminate the path forward, revealing the dance of risk and reward that characterizes the options trading landscape.

Definition and Mechanics of Call Options

a call option is a financial contract that provides the buyer the right, but not the obligation, to purchase a specific asset at a predetermined price (known as the strike price) within a fixed time frame. The sellers of call options, on the other hand, assume the obligation to sell the asset at the strike price if the buyer chooses to exercise the option.

Operational Mechanics

The allure of a call option lies in its leverage potential and flexibility. Here's a breakdown of its operational mechanics:

- Premium: The initiation of a call option requires the buyer to pay a premium to the seller. This premium is the price of acquiring the option and is influenced by various factors including the underlying asset's current price, the strike price, time until expiration, and market volatility.

- Strike Price: This is the agreed-upon price at which the asset can be bought. It is a crucial determinant of the option's profitability.

- Expiration Date: Call options come with an expiry date. The option must be exercised before this date, or it becomes worthless.

- Intrinsic and Time Value: The option's total value is derived from its intrinsic value (the difference between the underlying asset's current price and the strike price) and its time value, which diminishes as the expiration date approaches.

Strategic Significance

The strategic deployment of call options can serve multiple objectives within a trader's portfolio:

- Speculation: Traders optimistic about an asset's price increase might purchase call options to capitalize on this potential upswing with a relatively low capital investment compared to purchasing the asset outright.

- Hedging: Investors wanting to protect their holdings from a downturn in the market might use call options as a form of insurance, securing a sale price for assets they fear might depreciate in value.

- Income Generation: By selling call options on securities they own, investors can generate income through the premiums paid by buyers. This strategy, known as writing covered calls, provides an additional revenue stream while holding onto the assets.

Mechanics in Practice: An Example

To illustrate, consider a trader purchasing a call option on Company XYZ's stock, which is currently trading at $100. The option has a strike price of $105 and costs a $5 premium with an expiration date three months away. If, at expiration, XYZ's stock rises to $120, the trader can exercise the option to buy shares at $105, realizing a profit of $10 per share minus the initial $5 premium, effectively doubling the investment. Conversely, if the stock remains below $105, the option expires worthless, and the trader's loss is confined to the premium paid.

While call options can be employed as standalone instruments, their true potential is unleashed when integrated into sophisticated trading strategies. For example, in constructing an iron condor, call options are sold in conjunction with put options to establish a bounded range within which the trader anticipates the asset will remain through expiration.

Understanding call options is quintessential for traders aiming to navigate the volatile seas of the financial market with acumen. Their incorporation into broader trading strategies epitomizes the blend of analytical rigour and creative strategizing that marks the essence of successful trading.

Definition and Mechanics of Put Options

A put option is a contract that grants the holder the right, but not the obligation, to sell a specified quantity of an asset at a predetermined price (the strike price) before or on a specified expiration date. It's the mirror opposite of a call option, centering on anticipated declines in asset prices rather than increases.

Operational Mechanics

The mechanics of put options are governed by several key components, each contributing to the option's allure and strategic utility:

- Premium: The buyer of a put option pays a premium to the seller. This premium, determined by factors such as the asset's current price relative to the strike price, time until expiration, and market volatility, represents the cost of acquiring the put option.

- Strike Price: This critical element is the price at which the asset can be sold under the option contract. It is a pivotal factor in determining the option's profit potential.

- Expiration Date: Put options carry an expiry date, marking the window within which the option can be exercised. Post this date, the option ceases to hold value.

- Intrinsic and Time Value: Similar to call options, a put option's value comprises its intrinsic value—reflecting the profit that could be realized if the option were exercised immediately—and its time value, which gradually erodes as the expiration date approaches.

Strategic Significance

Put options serve versatile strategic purposes within an investor's arsenal:

- Speculation on Declines: Traders anticipating a downturn in an asset's price might purchase put options to profit from the forecasted decline with a comparatively minimal initial outlay.

- Hedging Against Downside Risk: Investors can utilize put options to safeguard their portfolios against potential losses, essentially insuring the value of their holdings.

- Income through Option Writing: By selling put options, investors can generate income in the form of premiums, especially in a stable or rising market where the likelihood of the option being exercised is lower.

Mechanics in Practice: An Illustrative Example

Imagine an investor acquiring a put option on Company ABC's stock, currently valued at $100, with a strike price of $90 for a $5 premium, expiring in three months. If ABC's stock plummets to $75, the investor can exercise the option to sell at $90, realizing a profit of $15 per share, minus the $5 premium paid. This scenario highlights the protective potential of put options against market downturns. Conversely, should the stock price not dip below $90, the option expires worthless, with the investor's loss limited to the premium paid.

Beyond standalone use, put options are integral to sophisticated trading strategies such as protective puts for downside protection, or combined with call options in straddles and strangles to bet on volatility without a clear directional bias. In the context of iron condors, put options are sold alongside call options to form a position that profits from stability in the underlying asset's price.

Mastering the dynamics of put options is indispensable for traders and investors aiming to fortify their market positions against uncertainties. The judicious application of put options, both in isolation and within complex strategies, embodies the confluence of tactical foresight and risk management essential to navigating the financial markets' ebbs and flows.

How Prices are Determined: Supply, Demand, and Volatility

Economic theory lies the principle of supply and demand, a concept as applicable to the bustling world of financial markets as it is to the simplest marketplace. The price of an asset, be it a stock, a bond, or a commodity, is fundamentally determined by the balance (or imbalance) between how much of it is available (supply) and how much of it traders want to buy (demand).

- Supply: This refers to the quantity of a particular asset that is available for purchase at any given time. An increase in supply, all else being equal, tends to push prices down, as sellers may accept lower offers to off-load their holdings.

- Demand: Conversely, demand measures how much desire there is among traders and investors to own an asset. Higher demand, against a static or dwindling supply, drives prices up, as buyers are willing to pay more to secure their desired shares or commodities.

The interplay of supply and demand is visible in the stock market when companies issue new shares (increasing supply) or buy back existing ones (reducing supply). Similarly, a surge in investor interest can increase demand, pushing prices higher.

Volatility: The Wildcard of Price Dynamics

Volatility introduces an element of unpredictability and risk into the market, serving as a measure of the price movements of an asset over a given period. High volatility indicates that an asset's price can change dramatically in a short amount of time in either direction, which can be the result of:

- Market Sentiment: The collective mood or attitude of investors towards a particular asset or the market in general can cause rapid price shifts.

- Economic Indicators: Reports on employment, inflation, and other economic fundamentals can sway market sentiment and, consequently, prices.

- Geopolitical Events: Elections, trade wars, and geopolitical tensions can lead to uncertainty, influencing investors to buy or sell, which impacts volatility and prices.

Volatility itself can become a commodity, with traders speculating on future price movements rather than the underlying asset's utility. This speculative aspect adds another layer to the already complex process of price determination.

An Illustrative Example: A Tale of Two Commodities

Consider the case of two commodities: oil and gold. The price of oil might plummet due to a decision by major producing countries to increase output (a supply surge) or a downturn in the global economy reducing demand for energy. Conversely, gold, often seen as a safe haven during times of economic uncertainty, might see its price rise amidst the same economic downturn as investors flock to it, increasing demand even if the supply remains constant.

Integrating Supply, Demand, and Volatility into Trading Strategies

For traders, understanding these principles is not merely academic; it's a critical component of strategy development. By analyzing supply and demand dynamics, a trader can anticipate potential price movements. Similarly, by assessing volatility, traders can gauge risk and potential reward. This understanding is crucial when employing strategies like iron condors, where the goal is to profit from an asset's price stability, or when navigating options trading, where volatility can significantly impact premiums.

The determination of prices in the financial markets is a complex dance of supply, demand, and volatility. Each factor plays a crucial role, and their interplay determines the ever-changing landscape in which traders operate. Mastery of these concepts enables traders to navigate the markets with greater confidence and strategic acumen, positioning them to capitalize on opportunities and mitigate risks.

Basics of Options Trading Strategies

Before delving into strategies, it's crucial to understand the two primary instruments in options trading: call options and put options.

- Call Options grant the holder the right, but not the obligation, to purchase an underlying asset at a predetermined price (the strike price) within a specified time frame. Traders buy call options when they anticipate the asset's price will rise, aiming to buy at a price lower than the market will offer in the future.

- Put Options afford the holder the right, but not the obligation, to sell an underlying asset at the strike price before the option expires. Traders utilize put options to hedge against potential declines in the underlying asset's price or to speculate on such declines.

Covered Calls for Income Generation

One of the most straightforward strategies is the covered call, where a trader owns the underlying asset and sells call options on the same asset. The goal is to generate income through the option premiums paid by the buyers. This strategy benefits from stable to slightly rising markets but carries the risk of limited profit potential should the underlying asset's price surge.

Conversely, the protective put strategy involves holding a long position in an asset while buying put options on the same asset. This approach serves as an insurance policy, protecting against significant downturns. It's akin to having a safety net, allowing the trader to participate in the upside while mitigating downside risk.

The straddle strategy involves buying a call option and a put option on the same asset, with the same strike price and expiration date. Traders employ straddles when they anticipate substantial price movement but are uncertain of the direction. This strategy profits from high volatility but comes at the cost of the premiums paid for both options.

An iron condor is a more advanced strategy, constructed by selling one out-of-the-money put, buying one out-of-the-money put with a lower strike price, selling one out-of-the-money call, and buying one out-of-the-money call with a higher strike price. All options have the same expiration date. This strategy aims to profit from markets that move little, capturing premium income as the options sold expire worthless. The risk lies in the potential for significant market moves that can lead to losses beyond the premiums received.

In all options trading strategies, risk management is paramount. Understanding the potential for loss and employing strategies to mitigate that risk—such as setting stop-loss orders or adjusting positions in response to market movements—is critical to long-term success.

Options provide a powerful toolkit for traders, capable of adapting to nearly any market scenario. Whether seeking to generate income, protect against losses, or capitalize on volatility, there is an options strategy to suit. However, with their complexity and inherent risks, a deep understanding of each strategy's mechanics, along with thorough market analysis and a robust risk management plan, is essential for any trader looking to navigate the options market successfully.

Traders lay the foundation upon which they can build more complex strategies, tailor strategies to fit their market outlook and risk tolerance, and navigate the options market with confidence.

Bullish vs. Bearish Strategies

In the theater of options trading, bullish and bearish strategies represent the two fundamental outlooks traders adopt based on their market sentiment. These strategies are tailored to leverage the anticipated upward or downward movements in asset prices. Understanding the distinction, application, and risk associated with each is pivotal for traders aiming to align their portfolios with forecasted market trends.

Bullish strategies are employed when a trader believes that the market or a specific asset will experience an upward trajectory. These strategies are designed to profit from increases in asset prices, with varying degrees of risk exposure and profit potential.

The long call strategy involves buying call options with the expectation that the underlying asset will increase in value. This approach offers unlimited profit potential, with losses limited to the premium paid for the options. The simplicity and straightforward profit mechanism make it a go-to strategy for many bullish traders.

The bull call spread strategy involves buying a call option while simultaneously selling another call option with a higher strike price but the same expiration date. This strategy reduces the upfront cost (premium paid) by offsetting it with the premium received from selling the call option. The profit potential is capped, but so is the risk, making it a balanced approach for modest bullish outlooks.

Conversely, bearish strategies are utilized when a trader anticipates a downturn in the market or a specific asset. These strategies aim to profit from declines in asset prices, with each strategy offering different risk-reward profiles.

The long put strategy is the mirror image of the long call, where a trader buys put options on an asset they expect to decrease in value. The potential profit is significant if the asset price falls below the strike price, limited only by the asset reaching zero value. The maximum loss is restricted to the premium paid for the put options.

In a bear put spread, a trader buys put options at a certain strike price and sells the same number of puts at a lower strike price. This strategy is employed to benefit from a moderate decline in the underlying asset's price. The sale of the lower strike put helps offset the cost of the puts purchased, reducing the total investment and risk. However, this also means the profit potential is capped.

Regardless of the market outlook, effective risk management underpins successful trading strategies. This involves setting clear objectives, determining tolerance levels for gains and losses, and employing stop-loss orders or protective puts to safeguard investments. Additionally, diversification across strategies can mitigate the risk of significant losses.

Savvy traders continuously monitor market conditions and are prepared to modify their strategies in response to new information or changes in market sentiment. This adaptability can involve switching between bullish and bearish strategies or adjusting the strike prices and expiration dates of options to better align with current market forecasts.

Bullish and bearish strategies in options trading offer traders tools to speculate on or hedge against future price movements of assets. By understanding and applying these strategies judiciously, traders can navigate the complexities of the market, tapping into opportunities presented by both rising and falling markets. However, the hallmark of successful trading lies not just in selecting the right strategy but also in managing risk, adapting to changing market conditions, and maintaining a disciplined approach to trading.

Neutral Strategies: Where Iron Condors Fit

Neutral strategies are predicated on the expectation that the underlying asset will not experience significant price movement within a specific timeframe. These strategies are especially appealing in markets characterized by low volatility, where predictability is higher compared to the tumultuous phases of bullish or bearish trends.

The Iron Condor strategy is a sophisticated orchestration of four different option contracts, creating a position that can profit from a range-bound market. This strategy involves selling one out-of-the-money put, buying another put with a lower strike price, selling an out-of-the-money call, and buying another call with a higher strike price. The alignment of these positions forms a configuration with limited risk and a defined profit potential within a specific range.

To construct an Iron Condor, a trader creates two vertical

spreads—a put spread and a call spread—with both spreads out of the money. This dual approach capitalizes on the decay of option premiums over time, assuming the underlying asset's price does not breach the strikes of the outer options. The distance between the strikes determines the risk/reward ratio of the strategy, guiding the trader's potential profit and loss.

For the Iron Condor strategy to unfold its wings to success, the underlying asset must remain within a certain price range, allowing all options involved to expire worthless. This ideal scenario grants the trader the maximum profit, which is the net premium received from setting up the Iron Condor. However, rigorous attention must be paid to the selection of strike prices and expiration dates, as these factors critically influence the strategy's viability.

The appeal of Iron Condors lies in their predefined risk and potential for consistent returns in low-volatility environments. However, the strategy is not without its perils. A significant move in the underlying asset beyond the established range could erode profits or incur losses. Therefore, adept management and an acute awareness of market signals are indispensable for navigating these risks effectively.

A distinctive advantage of Iron Condors is the possibility for adjustments. Should the market begin to edge towards one of the strategy's boundaries, a trader can make preemptive adjustments to mitigate losses or protect profits. These adjustments might include rolling out positions to different strikes or expiration dates, thus realigning the strategy with the evolving market landscape.

Neutral strategies, and Iron Condors in particular, offer a methodical approach to options trading that aligns with specific market conditions. By crafting positions that benefit from stagnation rather than dramatic shifts, traders can extract value from phases of market calm. Mastery of the Iron Condor strategy requires a blend of strategic foresight, risk management, and adaptability—qualities that, once honed, can significantly enhance a trader's portfolio. In options trading, where volatility often reigns, the Iron Condor strategy emerges as a testament to the power of equilibrium, providing a path to profit in the eye of the storm.

Risk Management Fundamentals

The inception point of any risk management strategy involves a comprehensive understanding of the types of risks inherent in options trading. Market risk, liquidity risk, and counterparty risk form the triumvirate that demands constant vigilance. Market risk pertains to the fluctuations in asset prices, liquidity risk to the ease of entering and exiting positions without affecting the market price, and counterparty risk to the possibility of a trading partner defaulting on their obligation.

A cardinal rule in risk management is the alignment of trading activities with one's risk tolerance and capacity. Risk tolerance is a subjective measure of an investor's comfort with uncertainty and potential financial loss. Risk capacity, on the other hand, refers to the objective amount of risk one can afford to take, considering financial goals and obligations. Balancing these aspects ensures that a trader does not venture beyond their means or comfort zone.

Diversification stands as a timeless strategy, mitigating risk by spreading investments across various assets or strategies. In the context of Iron Condor trading, diversification can be applied by varying strike prices, expiration dates, and underlying assets.

This tactic buffers the portfolio against significant losses, as not all investments are likely to move in the same direction simultaneously.

The deployment of stop-loss orders is a tactical measure to curtail losses. By establishing a specific price at which a position is automatically closed, traders can limit their exposure to unforeseen market downturns. It's a balancing act; setting these parameters too tight might lead to premature exit from potentially profitable positions, while too loose a setting could result in substantial losses.

Effective risk management is not a set-it-and-forget-it affair but a dynamic process that requires continuous monitoring and adjustments. Market conditions, economic indicators, and geopolitical events can swiftly alter the risk landscape. Regularly reviewing positions and making necessary adjustments ensures that the Iron Condor strategy remains aligned with risk parameters and market realities.

An often-overlooked aspect of risk management is the trader's psychological resilience. The emotional rollercoaster of trading —experiencing both wins and losses—can lead to decision fatigue, overconfidence, or the fear of missing out (FOMO), each of which can cloud judgment. Cultivating a mindset that remains detached from short-term outcomes, focusing instead on long-term strategy and discipline, fortifies traders against these psychological pitfalls.

Stress testing involves simulating extreme market conditions to evaluate how a trading strategy would perform under duress. This exercise unveils potential vulnerabilities in the Iron Condor setup and allows traders to recalibrate their strategies proactively. Whether it's a sudden market crash, skyrocketing volatility, or unexpected geopolitical events, stress testing prepares traders for the unforeseen, enabling them to navigate tumultuous waters with confidence.

Risk management is the unsung hero in the narrative of options trading success. It's the disciplined application of these fundamentals that arms traders with the capability to persevere through market vicissitudes, safeguarding their capital. For practitioners of the Iron Condor strategy, embracing these risk management principles is not just a choice but a necessity, laying the groundwork for achieving sustainable financial objectives and cultivating a resilient trading methodology.

The Importance of Volatility

Volatility embodies the dynamic heart of the markets, pulsating with each tick of the trading clock. It is this heartbeat that options traders must attune their strategies to. High volatility environments often signal increased risk, as the price of the underlying asset can swing widely, potentially breaching the bounds of an Iron Condor's wings. Conversely, low volatility suggests a more stable market, but with narrower profit margins, as premium incomes from selling options diminish.

Navigating the volatile waters of options trading requires a compass, which comes in the form of historical and implied volatility. Historical volatility calculates the past variance of price movements, offering a rearview mirror into the asset's temperamental history. This backward-looking measure, while informative, is complemented by implied volatility, which peers into the market's crystal ball, inferring future fluctuations based on current option prices. For the Iron Condor strategist, the interplay between these two forms of volatility is crucial. Implied volatility, in particular, serves as a gauge for setting appropriate strike prices and expiry dates, optimizing the strategy's potential profitability against anticipated market movements.

The quintessence of the Iron Condor strategy lies in its quest for balance; it thrives in a market that neither soars too high nor plunges too deep. Volatility directly influences this equilibrium. An unexpected spike in volatility can widen the spread between strike prices, increasing the risk of one side of the condor being breached, thereby eroding profits. On the flip side, should volatility plummet, the premiums collected from the options sold may not suffice to cover the trade's potential losses or transaction costs, squeezing the profitability window.

The concept of volatility skew is paramount for options traders. It refers to the pattern that implied volatility tends to be higher for lower strike prices, reflecting the market's greater fear of dramatic declines over spikes. This skew affects Iron Condor positions, as the disparity in implied volatility between the call and put spreads can impact pricing and risk assessment. Savvy traders must adjust their strike selection and hedging strategies to accommodate this skew, ensuring that both wings of the condor are balanced not just in price but in perceived risk.

Mastering volatility entails not just understanding its mechanics but also leveraging its predictive power. One advanced tactic involves timing the entry of an Iron Condor trade to coincide with historical patterns of volatility cycles. For instance, entering a trade after a period of high volatility may capitalize on the subsequent contraction, as markets tend to revert to mean levels of fluctuation. Furthermore, monitoring events known to trigger volatility—such as earnings announcements, economic data releases, and geopolitical developments—can inform the strategic adjustment of positions or the temporary avoidance of trades altogether.

volatility stands as a central pillar in the architecture of options trading strategies, particularly for those wielding the Iron Condor. Its understanding and strategic application are what transform an ordinary trader into a volatility virtuoso. By meticulously analyzing historical and implied volatility, adjusting for volatility skews, and timing trades around volatility cycles, the Iron Condor trader can navigate the tempests of market fluctuation. This mastery over volatility not only mitigates risks but also elevates the potential for sustainable profits, solidifying the Iron Condor's reputation as a strategy of finesse in the options trading arena.

Historical vs. Implied Volatility

Historical volatility, often referred to as statistical volatility, measures the rate at which the price of an underlying asset has moved in the past over a specific time frame. Calculated as the standard deviation of daily price changes, it provides a quantified snapshot of past market behavior, offering insights into the asset's stability or turbulence during the observed period. For traders, historical volatility is a valuable tool for understanding an asset's temperament, aiding in the assessment of risk associated with potential trades.

The utility of historical volatility in the Iron Condor strategy lies in its ability to inform traders about the asset's previous behavior patterns. By analyzing these patterns, traders can make educated guesses about future volatility trends, adjusting their strategies accordingly. For example, if an asset demonstrates a cyclical pattern of volatility, a trader might time the placement of an Iron Condor to align with expected periods of lower volatility, thereby reducing the risk of breaching the strategy's price boundaries.

Implied volatility stands on the other end of the spectrum, representing the market's expectation of how volatile an asset will be in the future. Unlike historical volatility, which is backward-looking, implied volatility is forward-looking, derived from the pricing of options themselves. It reflects the collective sentiment of the market participants regarding the anticipated magnitude of price movements of the underlying asset.

Implied volatility is crucial for options traders, particularly for those employing strategies like the Iron Condor, as it directly impacts options pricing. Higher implied volatility typically leads to higher option premiums, making it a critical factor in selecting strike prices and expiry dates. Traders use implied volatility to gauge whether an option is relatively cheap or expensive, thus influencing their selling and buying decisions. Moreover, changes in implied volatility can affect the profitability of an Iron Condor position, even if the underlying asset's price remains within the strategy's profit range.

Understanding the dynamic interplay between historical and implied volatility is essential for Iron Condor traders. While historical volatility offers a glimpse into the asset's past price fluctuations, implied volatility provides a speculative view of its future volatility. This distinction is critical because an asset with a history of stable price movement (low historical volatility) may suddenly become subject to market forces that lead to expectations of greater price swings (high implied volatility), affecting options pricing and strategy outcomes.

Traders often compare historical and implied volatility to identify discrepancies or convergences that may signal trading opportunities. For instance, if implied volatility is significantly higher than historical volatility without a clear reason, options may be overpriced, presenting a selling opportunity for Iron Condor traders. Conversely, if implied volatility is unusually low compared to historical volatility, it may indicate underpricing of options, suggesting a buying opportunity.

In practice, successful Iron Condor traders continuously monitor both historical and implied volatility to refine their strategies. They look for discrepancies between the two as potential indicators of market sentiment shifts. By leveraging these insights, traders can better position their Iron Condors to capitalize on expected market conditions, enhancing their potential for profit while managing the risks posed by volatility.

Moreover, understanding the nuanced relationship between historical and implied volatility enables traders to make informed decisions regarding the adjustment of their positions in response to changes in market expectations. Whether it's deciding to close out positions Early, repositioning the strikes or adjusting the width of the spreads, the informed interpretation of volatility metrics can significantly influence the strategic management of Iron Condor trades.

The juxtaposition of historical and implied volatility forms a foundational pillar in the architecture of options trading strategies, particularly the Iron Condor. Mastery of these concepts allows traders to navigate the ebbs and flows of market sentiment, positioning themselves to exploit volatility for strategic advantage. Through a deep understanding of both historical patterns and market expectations, traders can optimize their approach, balancing the pursuit of profit with the imperative of risk management. This nuanced grasp of volatility not only illuminates the path to successful trading but also deepens the trader's engagement with the ever-changing tapestry of the financial markets.

Volatility Smiles and Skews

The term "volatility smile" refers to a graphical representation where implied volatility is plotted against various strike prices for options with the same maturity. The result is often a curve that resembles a smile, with implied volatility typically lower for at-the-money (ATM) options and higher for in-the-money (ITM) and out-of-the-money (OTM) options. This pattern indicates that the market anticipates larger price movements for the underlying asset, leading to higher implied volatilities for options that are far from the current market price.

For Iron Condor traders, the volatility smile presents a nuanced landscape. The elevated implied volatilities at the wings of the smile (ITM and OTM options) suggest that the premiums for these options could be more substantial, potentially enhancing the profitability of an Iron Condor strategy if the underlying asset's price remains stable. However, this also implies a market expectation of significant price movement, which could introduce greater risk to the strategy if the asset price moves aggressively, breaching the Iron Condor's boundaries.

Volatility Skews: Asymmetry in Perception

Volatility skew, on the other hand, refers to the observed pattern where implied volatilities vary not in a symmetrical smile but in a skewed manner across strike prices. Commonly, this skew is seen as a tilt towards higher volatilities for OTM put options compared to ATM or ITM options, reflecting a market inclination towards anticipating significant downward movements in the underlying asset's price.

The presence of a volatility skew is particularly relevant for Iron Condor traders as it highlights an asymmetry in market expectations. The higher implied volatility for OTM puts suggests that protective puts are in demand, possibly due to bearish sentiment or hedging activities. For the Iron Condor trader, this skew can influence the selection of strike prices for the put spread component of the strategy, impacting both risk exposure and potential return. Engaging with a market characterized by a pronounced volatility skew requires a keen understanding of market sentiment and the factors driving demand for downside protection.

Strategic Considerations and Actions

Navigating the nuances of volatility smiles and skews demands a strategic approach from the Iron Condor trader. Key considerations include:

- Strike Price Selection: Analyzing the shape of the volatility smile or skew can guide the selection of strike prices for the Iron Condor's call and put spreads. Traders might opt for strike prices in regions with relatively lower implied volatilities to enhance premium collection, balanced against the risk of price movements breaching the spreads.

- Market Sentiment Analysis: Volatility smiles and skews reflect underlying market sentiments and expectations. Traders should integrate this information with other market analysis and indicators to gauge the broader market mood and potential directional biases.

- Adjustment Strategies: In markets exhibiting strong volatility smiles or skews, Iron Condor traders may need to employ more dynamic adjustment strategies. This could involve closer monitoring of positions, readying to make timely adjustments or close positions to manage risk effectively.

- Premium Considerations: The elevated implied volatilities at the extremes of smiles and skews suggest potentially higher premiums available for certain options. Traders must weigh these opportunities against the increased risk of significant price movements implied by these volatility patterns.

Understanding and strategically responding to volatility smiles and skews are imperative for traders employing the Iron Condor strategy. These patterns offer a window into market expectations and sentiment, informing decisions from strike price selection to risk management. By adeptly navigating volatility smiles and skews, traders can refine their strategies, aligning them more closely with market realities and enhancing their potential for success in the world of options trading.

How Volatility Affects Iron Condor Positions

Volatility represents the degree of variation in the price of an asset over time; it is a measure of uncertainty or risk. For options, volatility is a critical factor influencing premiums, where higher volatility generally equates to higher premiums, and vice versa. This relationship is pivotal for Iron Condor traders, for whom the premium collected upfront is the bedrock of potential profits.

Volatility's Dual Edged Sword on Iron Condors

The Iron Condor strategy thrives in environments of low to

moderate volatility, where the underlying asset's price oscillates within a predictable range, allowing the position to expire worthless and the trader to retain the maximum premium. However, volatility's fluctuating nature means the serene seas in which Iron Condors sail can swiftly turn tempestuous.

1. Increased Volatility: A surge in volatility can dramatically affect Iron Condor positions by widening the range of potential price movement. This heightened uncertainty can erode the value of the position as the likelihood of the underlying asset's price breaching the Iron Condor's boundaries increases. Furthermore, increased volatility can inflate option premiums, making adjustments or closings of positions more costly for the trader.

2. Decreased Volatility: Conversely, a decline in volatility can fortify an Iron Condor position, reducing the price movement's potential range and thereby the risk of breaching the strategy's bounds. Lower volatility can lead to a decrease in option premiums, potentially enabling profitable adjustments or the early closing of positions at a reduced cost.

Navigating Volatility: Strategic Implications for Iron Condor Traders

Understanding the impact of volatility necessitates a proactive and adaptive approach to managing Iron Condor positions. Traders must remain vigilant, ready to adjust their sails as the winds of volatility shift. Key strategies include:

- Volatility Monitoring: Keeping a close eye on volatility indicators, such as the VIX (Volatility Index), provides insights into market sentiment and potential volatility shifts, enabling traders to anticipate and react to changes that could impact their positions.

- Adjustment Techniques: In the face of increasing volatility, traders may need to employ adjustment strategies, such as rolling out positions to further expirations or adjusting strike prices to manage risk and protect potential profits.

- Entry and Exit Timing: Selecting the optimal time to enter or exit an Iron Condor position is crucial. Entry during periods of relatively high implied volatility can result in higher premiums collected, whereas seeking to close or adjust positions before volatility spikes can safeguard against unwelcome losses.

- Diversification: Spreading Iron Condor positions across different underlying assets or timeframes can mitigate the risk associated with volatility spikes in any single market, providing a buffer against unforeseen market movements.

Mastering the Volatility Dance

Volatility's impact on Iron Condor positions is profound, with its fluctuations capable of both elevating and undermining the strategy's effectiveness. By embracing volatility as a constant companion, rather than a foe, Iron Condor traders can navigate the tumultuous seas of options trading with greater confidence and agility. Through vigilant monitoring, strategic adjustments, and judicious timing, traders can harness volatility's power, turning its challenges into opportunities for refinement and growth in the art of options strategy.

The Iron Condor Strategy Explained

At its essence, an Iron Condor is a non-directional options trading strategy designed to profit when the underlying security experiences low volatility. The strategy involves the simultaneous opening of a bull put spread and a bear call spread on the same underlying asset with the same expiration date. This configuration encapsulates the trader's expectation into a range-bound bet, where profits are maximized if the underlying asset stays within a specified price range.

The Mechanics: Constructing an Iron Condor

Constructing an Iron Condor requires a deliberate and precise approach. The strategy is composed of four options contracts:

1. Selling an Out-of-the-Money (OTM) Call: This option has a strike price above the current price of the underlying asset. It represents the upper boundary of the desired range.

2. Buying an OTM Call: With a higher strike price than the sold call, this option serves as a hedge, capping the maximum potential loss on the upper side.

3. Selling an OTM Put: This option has a strike price below the current price of the underlying asset, forming the lower boundary of the range.

4. Buying an OTM Put: With a lower strike price than the sold put, this contract limits the downside risk, completing the protective framework of the Condor.

The combination of these options creates a net credit to the trader's account; this credit represents the maximum potential profit of the strategy.

Navigating Through Market Volatility

The Iron Condor is a champion in times of low volatility, but its robustness is tested as the market mood swings. The key to maintaining the Iron Condor's integrity lies in the trader's ability to anticipate and react to shifts in volatility:

- Adjustment Strategies: Traders can adjust the positions by shifting the strike prices of the spreads or by rolling the entire Condor to a later expiration date, seeking to navigate away from immediate threats and towards more tranquil waters.

- Exit Plans: Sometimes, the most prudent strategy is to exit the position, either partially or entirely, to preserve capital or lock in gains. This decision hinges on a clear-eyed assessment of evolving market conditions and the potential for recovering or enhancing the position's profitability.

The Psychological Dimension

The Iron Condor strategy is as much a psychological endeavor as a technical one. The trader must cultivate patience, discipline, and an unshakeable calm, traits that are indispensable in the face of market unpredictability. Success with Iron Condors is not measured by the outcome of a single trade but by the consistency of performance over time.

Mastery of the Iron Condor does not come overnight. It demands a deep understanding of options theory, a keen eye for market analysis, and an unwavering commitment to disciplined risk management. The journey to proficiency involves a continuous cycle of learning, application, and reflection, with each trade serving as a stepping stone to greater insight and expertise.

The Iron Condor strategy, with its elegant structure and strategic depth, offers traders a powerful tool for generating returns in low-volatility environments. By mastering its intricacies, traders can elevate their trading repertoire, navigating the markets with a blend of analytical precision and strategic acumen. In options trading, the Iron Condor stands as a testament to the harmony of knowledge, strategy, and psychological fortitude, guiding traders towards the pinnacle of trading mastery.

CHAPTER 2: THE IRON CONDOR STRATEGY EXPLAINED

An Iron Condor is essentially a combination of two options spreads: a put spread and a call spread. These spreads are constructed by selling and buying options with different strike prices but the same expiration date. The beauty of this strategy lies in its ability to generate profit from minimal market movement, positioning it as an ideal tactic for markets experiencing low volatility.

The strategy earns its name from the visual resemblance of its profit and loss graph to the majestic wingspan of a condor. The "wings" are formed by the sold and bought options, designed to limit potential losses. Let's dissect the components:

1. Selling an Out-of-the-Money Put: This is the first wing. You sell a put option at a strike price lower than the current market price. This position is profitable if the market stays above this strike price.

2. Buying an Out-of-the-Money Put: To protect against

significant downside movement, you buy a put option with a strike price even lower than the sold put. This defines your potential loss on the downside.

3. Selling an Out-of-the-Money Call: The second wing takes flight here. You sell a call option with a strike price higher than the market price, profiting if the market remains below this level.

4. Buying an Out-of-the-Money Call: To cap potential losses on the upside, you buy a call option with a strike price higher than the sold call. This action delineates your maximum loss on the upper side.

The area between the sold options represents the body of the Iron Condor and is where the potential for profit lies. If the market price at expiration falls within this range, all options will expire worthless, allowing the trader to retain the premiums collected at the outset.

The trader's maximum profit is the net premium received after accounting for the cost of the bought options. Conversely, the maximum risk is the difference between the strike prices of the bought and sold options, minus the net premium received.

Achieving success with the Iron Condor requires a delicate balance. The wider the distance between the strike prices, the greater the maximum profit but also the higher the risk of the price moving beyond one of the sold options. Conversely, a narrower distance reduces potential profit but also limits risk.

The Iron Condor thrives in a market with low volatility, where prices fluctuate within a predictable range. It's a strategy that demands patience, precision, and an acute understanding of market sentiment. Traders must be adept at reading market signals, ready to adjust their positions in response to shifts in volatility or unexpected events.

The Iron Condor is not merely a trading strategy; it's a dance with the market, a test of foresight and adaptability. It offers a path to profit in stagnant markets, but like all strategies, it carries risks. A successful Iron Condor trader is one who meticulously plans, constantly observes the market's pulse, and respects the balance between risk and reward. This strategy is a powerful tool in the options trader's arsenal, offering a nuanced approach to earning in times of market tranquility.

Selling Out-of-the-Money Put Spread

An out-of-the-money put spread, often referred to as a bull put spread, involves two pivotal actions: selling a put option with a higher strike price and simultaneously buying a put option with a lower strike price. Both options share the same underlying asset and expiration date but differ in their strike prices. This spread is crafted with the anticipation that the underlying asset's price will remain above the strike price of the sold put, rendering both options worthless and allowing the trader to pocket the premium received.

1. Selection of the Sold Put: The first step is identifying the higher strike price at which to sell the put. This option should be out-of-the-money, meaning its strike price is below the current market price of the underlying asset. The choice of strike price is a delicate balance between seeking a sufficient premium and mitigating risk.

2. Selection of the Bought Put: The protective counterpart of the sold put is the bought put, which is selected with a strike price lower than that of the sold put. This option acts as a safety net, limiting maximum potential loss should the market move against the position.

3. Premium Consideration: The premium received for the sold put is higher than the cost of the bought put, resulting in a net premium that represents the maximum profit for this strategy. This net premium is the trader's to keep if both options expire worthless.

4. Risk Management: The maximum risk associated with an OTM put spread is the difference between the strike prices minus the net premium received. This risk is quantifiable and confined, making the spread a favored tactic among traders who seek defined risk parameters.

- Maximum Profit: Achieved when the price of the underlying asset remains above the strike price of the sold put at expiration. It is equal to the net premium received at the initiation of the spread.

- Maximum Loss: Occurs if the price of the underlying asset falls below the strike price of the bought put at expiration. It is the difference between the strike prices of the two puts, minus the net premium received.

- Breakeven Point: The breakeven for this strategy is the strike price of the sold put minus the net premium received. The asset's price must stay above this point at expiration for the trade to be profitable.

The decision to implement an OTM put spread is not taken in isolation but is a response to a trader's analysis of market conditions and volatility forecasts. This strategy is optimally deployed in a market where a moderate bullish sentiment prevails, or stability is anticipated. A successful trader navigates these conditions with a blend of analytical prowess and informed intuition, adjusting the spread parameters to align with evolving market narratives.

Selling Out-of-the-Money Call Spread

An out-of-the-money call spread, also known as a bear call spread, is crafted by selling a call option at a higher strike price while concurrently purchasing another call option with an even higher strike price. Both options operate under the same expiration timeline and engage the same underlying asset, yet they dance at differing strike prices. This strategic ensemble is orchestrated with the forecast that the underlying asset's price will not breach the strike price of the sold call, culminating in the options expiring worthless, thereby retaining the collected premium as profit.

1. Identifying the Sold Call: The initial step demands selecting a call option to sell, which should unequivocally be out-of-the-money. This means its strike price sits above the current market value of the underlying asset. The selection process is a balancing act, aiming to maximize the premium received while keeping an eye on risk exposure.

2. Choosing the Bought Call: The subsequent action involves picking a call option to buy, with its strike price loftier than that of the sold call. This option serves as a protective measure, capping the maximum loss should the market surge

unexpectedly.

3. Premium Dynamics: The premium garnered from the sold call surpasses the expenditure on the bought call, resulting in a net premium that epitomizes the strategy's maximum profit potential. This net premium, a trader's bounty, will be fully realized should both options graciously expire worthless.

4. Risk Containment: The maximal risk inherent in an OTM call spread is delineated by the difference in strike prices of the involved calls, less the net premium pocketed. This risk, though present, is finite and calculable, offering a safety net that appeals to the risk-averse trader.

- Peak Profit: Attained when the underlying asset's price lingers below the strike price of the sold call by expiration, the maximum profit equates to the initial net premium received.

- Utmost Loss: Manifests when the price of the underlying asset escalates above the strike price of the bought call by expiration. It is calculated as the disparity between the strike prices, subtracted by the net premium received.

- Breakeven Calculus: The breakeven point for this strategy is found by adding the net premium received to the strike price of the sold call. The market price must stay beneath this juncture at expiration for the position to accrue profit.

Implementing an OTM call spread is a strategic decision rooted in a trader's analysis and sentiment towards the market. This strategy finds its stride in a market landscape painted with moderate bearish hues or expected stagnation. It demands of the trader not just a keen analytical eye but also the agility to recalibrate strategy parameters in response to the shifting tides of market sentiment.

How These Components Create a Neutral Position

the Iron Condor lies a symphony of two distinct spreads: the OTM call spread and the OTM put spread. These components, by their nature, embody opposing market sentiments—bearish and bullish, respectively. Yet, when interwoven, they coalesce into a position that is uniquely insulated against the market's capricious movements, provided it remains within a predefined range.

1. OTM Call Spread: Positioned with the anticipation that the underlying asset will not exceed the higher strike price of the sold call option.

2. OTM Put Spread: Crafted under the premise that the underlying asset will not dip below the lower strike price of the sold put option.

The strategic juxtaposition of these elements leverages the market's tendency to fluctuate within a range over time, thus creating a neutral position that is primed for profitability in a stagnant or mildly volatile market scenario.

The essence of achieving neutrality through an Iron Condor strategy lies in the premium collected from the sale of the call and put spreads. The initial setup generates a net credit to the trader's account, representing the maximum potential profit of the strategy. This profit is fully realized if, at expiration, the underlying asset's price remains sandwiched between the strike prices of the sold options.

The structure inherently limits the maximum potential loss to the difference between the strike prices of the bought and sold options in either spread, minus the net premium received. This configuration ensures that while the strategy caps the profit potential, it simultaneously delineates and contains the risk exposure.

The equilibrium, or breakeven points, of an Iron Condor, are determined by adding the net premium received to the strike price of the sold put and subtracting it from the strike price of the sold call. These thresholds mark the boundaries within which the underlying asset's price must reside at expiration for the position to remain profitable.

- Upper Breakeven Point: Calculated by adding the net premium to the strike price of the sold call.

- Lower Breakeven Point: Found by subtracting the net premium from the strike price of the sold put.

Should the asset's price breach these points, the strategy begins to incur losses, maxing out if the price moves beyond the strike prices of the bought options.

The deployment of an Iron Condor is a testament to a trader's nuanced understanding of market sentiment and volatility. This strategy is particularly efficacious in a market exhibiting low to moderate volatility, where substantial price movements are unlikely within the strategy's duration. It is a premeditated wager on the market's inactivity or slight movements, drawing profits from the passage of time and the erosion of option premiums, known as theta decay.

While the Iron Condor is a model of market neutrality, it requires vigilant monitoring and an adaptive approach to manage effectively. Market movements toward either breakeven point may necessitate adjustments to the position to mitigate losses or lock in profits. These can include closing out one spread to reduce risk or adjusting strike prices to shift the breakeven points.

The Iron Condor strategy encapsulates a trader's skill in harnessing the market's innate undulations, crafting a position that finds its sweet spot in the equilibrium between bullish and bearish forces. It embodies a philosophical and tactical balance, a middle path that seeks profit in the market's tendency toward stasis rather than direction. Through the meticulous assembly of its components, the Iron Condor offers a nuanced route to profitability, one that is predicated on precision, patience, and a profound understanding of market dynamics.

Profit and Loss Potential

The Iron Condor strategy's profit potential is encapsulated in the premium received from the sale of the call and put spreads. This premium, a crystallization of the strategy's maximum profit, is pocketed by the trader at the inception of the trade. The fruition of this profit, however, hinges on a singular condition: the underlying asset's price must nestle within the boundaries defined by the strike prices of the sold options upon expiration.

The crux of maximising profit within an Iron Condor lies in the careful selection of strike prices and expiration dates, calibrated to balance the probability of the underlying asset's price remaining within the desired range against the premium received. The premium, serves as the trader's buffer against minor fluctuations in the market, with its size influenced by factors such as the width of the spreads and the prevailing market volatility.

While the Iron Condor is designed with a built-in mechanism to cap losses, understanding the contours of this spectrum is crucial for risk management. The maximum loss scenario materializes when the underlying asset's price breaches the boundaries and extends beyond the strike prices of the bought options. This delineation of loss is inherently tied to the distance between the strike prices within each spread—wider spreads imply a higher potential for loss, albeit accompanied by a larger premium, and vice versa.

The calculation of loss within an Iron Condor is straightforward yet vital for strategic planning:

- Maximum Loss: Equal to the difference between the strike prices of the bought and sold options within one spread, minus the initial premium received.

This equation underscores the Iron Condor's risk-reward equilibrium, with the strategy's structural integrity offering a shield against unlimited losses but necessitating astute management to mitigate potential financial setbacks.

The Iron Condor's allure lies in its capacity to generate returns in a range-bound market. However, its dual-edged nature demands vigilance and strategic foresight. Market conditions that precipitate heightened volatility can erode the strategy's profitability, propelling the underlying asset's price towards the breakeven points and beyond, into the terrain of losses.

Adjustments and tactical reconfigurations become the linchpins of sustaining the Iron Condor's equilibrium. Traders may opt to close or roll out parts of their position in response to unfavourable market movements, striving to salvage profits or curtail losses. Such maneuvers, while , are instrumental in the dynamic recalibration of the strategy in alignment with evolving market sentiments.

The Iron Condor strategy encapsulates a philosophical dialogue between risk and reward, a financial equipoise that leverages market neutrality in pursuit of profitability. It underscores the trader's journey through the volatile seas of options trading —a journey marked by calculated risks, strategic adjustments, and the perpetual quest for balance. The Iron Condor, with its defined profit and loss potentials, serves as a beacon for traders navigating the dynamics of the options market, offering a path to earnings that demands both respect for the market's forces and a nuanced understanding of its strategic deployment.

Maximum Loss Scenarios

Venturing deeper into the mechanics of the Iron Condor strategy, we confront the stark parameters of its maximum loss scenarios. This exploration is not merely an academic exercise but a practical foray into risk management within options trading. The Iron Condor, heralded for its structural elegance in balancing potential gains against losses, nevertheless harbors conditions under which the trader can incur maximal financial detriment. Here, we dissect these scenarios with precision, aiming not to dissuade the investor but to arm them with the knowledge necessary to navigate the tumultuous markets with acumen.

Central to understanding the Iron Condor's loss potential is the recognition of the pivotal role played by the strategy's outer wings—the bought options. The maximum loss is incurred when the market price of the underlying asset either plummets below the lower strike price of the put spread or soars above the upper strike price of the call spread at expiration. These are the thresholds at which the protective mechanisms of the Iron Condor falter, and the financial safeguards are breached.

The quantum of loss is not left to the whims of the market but is predefined by the strategy's configuration. The maximum loss is calculated as follows:

- Maximum Loss = (Width of the wider spread - Net Premium Received) × 100 (per contract)

This mathematical certainty provides a boundary to the unknown, offering a measure of solace amidst market unpredictability. The width of the spread between the bought and sold options delineates the risk exposure, with a wider spread indicating a larger area for potential loss, counterbalanced by a higher premium, providing a cushion against minor market movements.

1. Width of the Spreads: Wider spreads between the strike prices increase the maximum potential loss but also enhance the premium received, presenting a nuanced trade-off between risk and reward.

2. Market Volatility: High volatility periods inflate option premiums due to the increased uncertainty of price movement, impacting the net premium received and, consequently, the

maximum loss potential.

3. Time Decay: As expiration approaches, the time value of options diminishes. This temporal erosion can work in favor of the Iron Condor strategy by decreasing the value of the bought options, potentially mitigating losses if managed proactively.

The inherent beauty of the Iron Condor lies not in its invincibility but in its adaptability. Recognizing an impending maximum loss scenario beckons strategic responses:

- Adjustments: Early adjustments to the Iron Condor, such as rolling out the position to a further expiration or adjusting the strike prices, can be a salve to the wounds inflicted by adverse market movements.

- Defensive Exits: In some instances, the judicious choice to exit the position entirely before expiration, albeit at a loss, can prevent the maximum loss from crystallizing, preserving capital for future ventures.

Confronting the maximum loss scenarios of the Iron Condor strategy demands not only strategic acumen but also psychological resilience. The seasoned trader views these not as catastrophic endings but as integral components of a broader trading philosophy that embraces the probabilistic nature of the markets. It is within these challenging scenarios that the trader's mettle is tested, and their capacity for disciplined risk management is honed.

The Iron Condor strategy, with its clearly defined parameters for profit and loss, exemplifies the delicate art of equilibrium. Understanding and preparing for maximum loss scenarios is not a descent into pessimism but a strategic elevation towards informed, calculated trading. Thus armed, the trader can navigate the vicissitudes of the market with confidence, fortified by the knowledge that in the Iron Condor, the maximum loss, though unwelcome, is neither uncharted nor unconquerable.

The Importance of the Breakeven Point

At its essence, the breakeven point in options trading is the price level at which the trade neither makes nor loses money, excluding commissions or fees. Within Iron Condors, this concept metamorphoses into a dual-faceted entity, reflective of the strategy's dual spread structure. The breakeven points are thus found on both ends of the strategy's spectrum, enveloping the space within which profitability is poised.

The calculation of the breakeven points for an Iron Condor involves a straightforward addition and subtraction from the sold options, taking into account the net premium received. The formulas manifest as follows:

- Upper Breakeven Point = Strike Price of Sold Call + Net Premium Received

- Lower Breakeven Point = Strike Price of Sold Put - Net Premium Received

These calculations yield the thresholds that encapsulate the trader's profit zone. The expanse between these two points is the realm within which the market price of the underlying asset must reside at expiration for the trade to be profitable.

The breakeven points beacon the trader in several essential ways:

1. Trade Entry Criteria: Astutely set breakeven points can serve as critical criteria for entering a trade. They influence the selection of strike prices and the timing of trade execution, aligning with the trader's market outlook and risk tolerance.

2. Risk Assessment: The distance between the breakeven points and the current market price offers a tangible measure of the trade's risk exposure, providing a clear-eyed view of the potential for loss relative to the zone of profitability.

3. Performance Monitoring: As the market ebbs and flows, the breakeven points serve as milestones, guiding the trader's decisions on whether to adjust the trade, secure profits, or cut losses.

Navigating towards the breakeven points, the astute Iron Condor trader remains vigilant, ready to employ strategic adjustments should the market threaten these critical thresholds. Such adjustments, ranging from shifting the position's strike prices to extending its expiration, are predicated on the desire not merely to avoid loss but to realign the trade with evolving market realities, thus preserving the potential for profitability.

In the broader narrative of options trading, the breakeven point transcends its numerical essence, embodying a trader's journey towards equilibrium. It reflects the perpetual balance between fear and greed, risk and reward, movement and stasis. Mastering the dynamics of the breakeven point within the Iron Condor strategy is akin to mastering one's trading psyche, striking a harmonious chord between analytical rigor and intuitive foresight.

the breakeven points in the Iron Condor strategy are not merely numerical markers but strategic linchpins and philosophical beacons. They instruct, guide, and sometimes caution, embodying the dance between profit and loss. As traders navigate the complex terrain of options trading, understanding and respecting the breakeven point becomes indispensable, a testament to its immutable place in the annals of strategic trading.

Adjustments and Exit Strategies

Adjustments in the context of Iron Condor trading are strategic maneuvers undertaken to realign the position with the current market outlook, especially when the initial trade premise is threatened. These adjustments are not mere reactionary tactics but are premeditated actions, integrated into the trading plan from inception, ready to be deployed as the market narrative unfolds.

1. Adjusting for Market Movement: The most common trigger for adjustments is significant price movement towards one of the position's wings, threatening to breach a breakeven point. Here, traders might employ strategies such as rolling out the endangered wing to a further expiration date or adjusting the strike prices to widen the profit zone.

2. Defensive Adjustments: These are employed to reduce risk exposure, often by purchasing additional options that offset the delta of the original position. While such adjustments can

protect against adverse price movements, they also reduce the net premium and, by extension, the potential profitability of the trade.

3. Offensive Adjustments: Aimed at capitalizing on favorable market conditions, offensive adjustments might involve narrowing the spread between the strike prices to increase premium income, albeit at the expense of increased risk exposure.

An exit strategy in Iron Condors is a predetermined plan for closing the position, either to lock in profits or to cut losses. Such strategies hinge on specific criteria, including profit targets, loss thresholds, and time decay considerations.

1. Profit Target Exits: Setting a profit target is quintessential for any Iron Condor trader. Once a specific percentage of the maximum potential profit is achieved, the position is closed. This disciplined approach ensures that profits are secured without the greed-fueled temptation to hold for maximum gains, which could backfire should the market reverse.

2. Time-Based Exits: Given the Iron Condor's sensitivity to time decay, some traders opt for time-based exit strategies, particularly as expiration approaches. For instance, closing the position two weeks before expiration to avoid gamma risk—the risk of the option's delta changing rapidly.

3. Stop-Loss Exits: To prevent substantial losses, a trader might set a stop-loss level, typically a percentage of the trade's initial value. Upon reaching this threshold, the position is unwound, mitigating further financial detriment.

4. Conditional Exits: These involve closing the position based on specific market conditions or technical indicators, such as a breach of support or resistance levels.

The essence of adjustments and exit strategies lies not just in their technical execution but in their philosophical underpinnings. They embody the trader's adaptability, discipline, and foresight—qualities pivotal to navigating the unpredictable waters of options trading. Adjustments reflect the trader's resilience, a willingness to shift course in the face of market adversities. Conversely, exit strategies represent the culmination of discipline and detachment, the ability to part ways with a position when it no longer aligns with the market outlook or risk profile.

Adjustments and exit strategies are the lifelines of the Iron Condor strategy, essential tools in the trader's arsenal. They manifest the delicate balance between flexibility and firmness, between the pursuit of profit and the preservation of capital. Mastering these aspects is indispensable for any trader aspiring to harness the full potential of the Iron Condor, transforming it from a mere tactical play to a profound strategic endeavor in the vast arena of options trading.

Closing Parts of the Condor Early

The decision to close parts of an Iron Condor early is driven by several factors, each rooted in the trader's objective to optimize profitability while managing risk. These factors include significant market movements, imminent risk of loss breaching predetermined thresholds, and the capture of favorable premiums earlier than anticipated.

1. Market Sensitivity: The Iron Condor, being a market-neutral strategy, thrives in conditions of low volatility. However, abrupt market movements can destabilize this equilibrium. For example, a sudden bullish trend could threaten the call spread wing of the Condor. Proactively closing this part of the position can prevent potential losses and preserve the integrity of the overall strategy.

2. Risk Management: Every Iron Condor strategy is underpinned by a rigorous risk management protocol. Part of this approach involves setting loss limits. If the position starts to approach these limits due to unforeseen market dynamics, closing one or both parts of the Condor early can be a prudent step to stop the bleed.

3. Premium Capture: On occasions, the market may move in a manner that allows the trader to capture a significant portion of the maximum potential premium well before expiration. In such scenarios, closing the position early locks in profits and frees up capital for reinvestment.

Closing parts of an Iron Condor early requires a meticulous approach, blending analytical rigor with tactical agility.

1. Monitoring and Analysis: Continuous monitoring of the position and the market is vital. The use of real-time analytics and trading alerts can provide early warning signs necessitating an adjustment.

2. Partial Closure Techniques: When the decision to close early is made, it may involve buying back the sold options in the threatened wing of the Condor. This action neutralizes the risk

on that side of the trade while keeping the opposite side active, which may still generate profit.

3. Reassessment and Re-entry: After closing part of the Condor early, it's essential to reassess the market conditions. If the initial premise for the Iron Condor setup remains valid, the trader may consider re-entering the market with a new position adjusted to the current market realities.

The decision to close parts of an Iron Condor early is not without its consequences and implications.

1. Impact on Profitability: While early closure can protect against losses, it also impacts the overall profitability of the trade. The cost of buying back options and potential missed opportunities for full premium capture must be weighed against the benefits of risk mitigation.

2. Capital Allocation and Opportunity Cost: Closing a part of the Condor early frees up capital, which can be reallocated to other trading opportunities. However, this action must be considered within the context of opportunity costs and the comparative potential of alternative investments.

3. Psychological Considerations: The discipline to close a part of a trade early, particularly when facing an unfavorable market, is a testament to a trader's emotional control and risk management acumen. However, it requires a balanced mindset to avoid reactive or over-conservative decisions that might hamper potential gains.

Closing parts of an Iron Condor early is a nuanced strategy that balances the delicate interplay between profit optimization and risk management. It exemplifies the dynamic nature of options trading, where adaptability and disciplined decision-making are paramount. As traders navigate through the ever-changing market landscapes, the ability to make informed, timely adjustments such as these will be a cornerstone of sustained success in options trading. This strategic maneuver, when executed with precision, can significantly enhance the trader's ability to navigate the complexities of the market, turning potential threats into opportunities for financial growth and stability.

Using Stop Losses and Alerts

Stop losses and alerts serve as the sentinels of options trading, offering real-time protective measures against market adversities. Their importance in the context of Iron Condor trading cannot be overstated, for they provide:

1. Risk Limitation: By setting predefined stop loss points, traders can limit their potential losses to manageable levels, thus preventing catastrophic financial impacts from sudden market downturns.

2. Market Vigilance: Alerts keep traders apprised of market movements that could affect their positions, enabling swift, informed decision-making.

3. Emotional Equilibrium: The automated nature of stop losses can help traders maintain discipline, removing the emotional turmoil associated with manual exit decisions during volatile market conditions.

The tactical implementation of stop losses and alerts within an Iron Condor strategy is a nuanced process, demanding meticulous planning and precision.

1. Setting Stop Loss Points: Determining the stop loss level involves a careful analysis of the Iron Condor's risk-reward profile and the trader's risk tolerance. It's crucial to set these points at levels that balance potential losses with the opportunity for profitability, without prematurely exiting a position that could yet prove beneficial.

2. Configuring Alerts: Alerts should be set for price movements, volatility changes, and other market conditions that could impact the Iron Condor position. These alerts act as an early warning system, enabling traders to reassess their positions and make adjustments as necessary.

3. Platform Integration: Most trading platforms offer tools for setting stop losses and alerts. Traders must familiarize themselves with these tools, integrating them seamlessly into their trading strategy to ensure they function as intended.

While stop losses and alerts are indispensable tools in options trading, their deployment must be approached with consideration of several factors:

1. Gap Risk: Markets can move rapidly, sometimes 'gapping' past stop loss levels before the order can be executed. This possibility requires a strategy that considers the likelihood of such events and prepares for their financial implications.

2. Alert Overload: Setting too many alerts can lead to information overload, potentially causing paralysis by analysis. Traders need to strike the right balance, focusing on alerts that

provide actionable insights.

3. Adjustment Frequency: The dynamic nature of the market may necessitate frequent adjustments to stop loss levels and alert settings. This requires vigilance and a commitment to ongoing analysis.

The strategic use of stop losses and alerts is integral to navigating the complexities of Iron Condor trading with confidence and control. By judiciously implementing these tools, traders can protect their positions against sudden market movements, limit potential losses, and capitalize on opportunities with a disciplined, informed approach. This dual strategy of defense and vigilance epitomizes the calculated, proactive stance that distinguishes successful traders in the volatile arena of options trading.

Setting Up Your First Iron Condor

An Iron Condor is a non-directional options strategy that involves the simultaneous selling of a put spread and a call spread with the same expiration date but different strike prices. The goal is to profit from the underlying asset's price finishing within the two spreads at expiration, allowing the trader to retain the premium collected at the outset.

1. Selecting the Underlying Asset: The choice of the underlying asset is pivotal. Look for assets with high liquidity, as they ensure tighter bid-ask spreads and better pricing for your options. Indices or large-cap stocks often make ideal candidates for their stability and volume.

2. Market Condition Analysis: Iron Condors thrive in markets

exhibiting low to moderate volatility. Utilize historical volatility data alongside current market trends to identify periods of relative calm, which increase the probability of your Iron Condor expiring within the desired range.

3. Strike Price Selection: The selection of strike prices for both the call and put spreads is a delicate balance between risk and reward. Opt for out-of-the-money (OTM) options that provide a comfortable cushion against price movements while still offering a satisfactory premium.

4. Expiration Date Consideration: Shorter expiration periods typically favor Iron Condor strategies due to the accelerated time decay (Theta) of options. However, this must be weighed against the increased management frequency and potential for market movement. A 30-60 day expiration period often represents a reasonable compromise.

5. Monitoring for Entry Signals: Await a period of reduced volatility, using technical indicators or volatility indices as a guide. Patience during this stage is crucial; the right conditions can significantly impact the success rate of your strategy.

6. Position Sizing: Determine the size of your position based on your risk tolerance and capital allocation strategy. It's advisable to start small, allowing room for learning and adjustment.

7. Order Placement: Place your orders for both the put spread and call spread. It's often more effective to enter the position as a complete Iron Condor to ensure that all parts are filled at the desired prices.

8. Setting Initial Adjustments: Plan your adjustments in

advance. Should the market begin to move towards either of your spreads, have a predetermined strategy for rolling the threatened side to mitigate losses.

9. Use of Stop Losses: While Iron Condors are defined risk positions, setting stop loss levels can prevent significant drawdowns during unexpected market movements.

10. Regular Monitoring and Adjustment: Active management is key to maintaining a profitable Iron Condor position. Regularly assess the position's value and make adjustments as necessary to protect profits or reduce losses.

11. Exit Strategy: Know when to exit the trade, whether it's at a predetermined profit target, a stop loss level, or as expiration approaches. An effective exit strategy preserves capital and secures profits.

Setting up your first Iron Condor is both an exciting and demanding endeavor. It requires a blend of strategic planning, market insight, and disciplined risk management. By adhering to the principles outlined above, you are well-positioned to navigate the initial complexities of Iron Condor trading. Remember, success in options trading is not just about executing strategies but also about the continuous learning and adaptation that comes with experience. Your first Iron Condor is a significant step in a broader journey of financial education and trading mastery.

CHAPTER 3: SETTING UP YOUR FIRST IRON CONDOR

I n the quest to master the iron condor strategy, the initial step of selecting the right stock or index is akin to setting the sails in the correct direction before embarking on a maritime voyage. This decision, critical and foundational, dictates the journey's trajectory and potential success. The market's vast expanse offers a plethora of choices, each with its unique characteristics and underlying volatility, requiring a strategic approach to selection.

Understanding the Landscape

Before plunging into the mechanics of selection, one must comprehend the broader market landscape. Stocks, with their individual company narratives, present a tapestry of opportunities and risks, influenced by factors ranging from earnings reports to geopolitical events. Indices, on the other hand, offer a broader market exposure, aggregating the performance of select stocks to represent a segment of the financial market. This distinction is fundamental, as it underscores the difference between navigating the idiosyncrasies of single stocks and the aggregate movements of an index.

Central to the iron condor strategy is the concept of volatility. Volatility, both historical and implied, serves as the North Star, guiding traders in their selection process. Historical volatility reflects past price movements, offering a rearview mirror perspective. Implied volatility, however, peers into the future, encapsulating market expectations of price fluctuations. For an iron condor, a balanced approach to volatility is paramount. Too much volatility increases the risk of price movements breaching the strategy's boundaries, while too little diminishes the potential premium collected.

Liquidity, or the ease with which an asset can be bought or sold in the market without affecting its price, is the lifeblood of successful execution. In options trading, liquidity is reflected in the bid-ask spread—the difference between the highest price a buyer is willing to pay and the lowest price a seller is willing to accept. A narrower spread signifies higher liquidity, ensuring that positions can be entered and exited with minimal slippage. Selecting stocks or indices with high liquidity is thus crucial, as it facilitates smoother transactions and better pricing.

Earnings announcements and other significant market events are akin to tides in the ocean of the stock market—predictable yet capable of generating substantial waves. The anticipation of these events often inflates implied volatility, offering lucrative premiums for options traders. However, the actual event can lead to sharp price movements, threatening the safety margins of an iron condor. A savvy trader, therefore, approaches these periods with caution, often opting for positions in stocks or indices with upcoming events, but adjusting the strategy's parameters to account for the increased risk.

Consider the fictional XYZ Corporation, a tech giant known for its volatility around quarterly earnings announcements. A trader eyeing XYZ for an iron condor might decide to enter a position four weeks before the earnings release when implied volatility starts to rise, thereby capturing higher premiums. Alternatively, one might look to the S&P 500 index, a composite of leading U.S. companies, for a more diversified approach. The index's broad market representation and high liquidity make it an attractive candidate for traders seeking to minimize unsystematic risk.

Selecting the right stock or index for an iron condor strategy is a nuanced art, blending analysis of volatility, liquidity, and market events. By navigating these factors with a strategic lens, traders can set the sails of their iron condor strategy, aiming for a journey marked by calculated risk and potential reward. As with any voyage, the wisdom lies not in avoiding the sea but in mastering its currents.

Liquidity Considerations

Liquidity in the options market is quantified by the volume of trading and the tightness of the bid-ask spread. High trading volume ensures that there are ample buyers and sellers, facilitating smoother transaction flows. Meanwhile, a narrow bid-ask spread indicates that the cost of executing trades (the "market impact" cost) is lower, which is pivotal for strategies that entail frequent adjustments, such as the iron condor.

While assessing liquidity, traders must probe beyond superficial metrics. It's essential to evaluate the liquidity of both the options and the underlying stock or index. A highly liquid underlying asset does not automatically translate to liquidity in its options market. For instance, consider the fictional company "Tech Innovate" (TI), whose stocks enjoy high liquidity. However, its options might tell a different story, with wider bid-ask spreads and lower trading volumes, especially for contracts that are far out-of-the-money (OTM) or have distant expiration dates.

In the context of iron condors, liquidity assumes a dual significance. Firstly, it impacts the initial setup of the strategy, where entering positions at favorable prices is paramount to maximizing the potential profit. Secondly, liquidity is critical when adjusting or closing positions, especially in response to market movements. Illiquid options may force traders to accept unfavorable prices, eroding the strategy's profitability.

Let's consider a practical scenario involving the S&P 500 index (SPX), renowned for its deep liquidity. A trader looking to implement an iron condor strategy on SPX options would benefit from the narrower bid-ask spreads and high trading volumes, enabling efficient entry and adjustment of positions. Contrarily, applying the same strategy on a less liquid ETF might result in significant slippage, undermining the strategy's effectiveness.

Traders can adopt several tactics to mitigate liquidity risk in their iron condor strategies. One effective approach is to limit strategies to highly liquid underlying assets and options. This might mean focusing on major indices like the SPX or on stocks with robust options markets. Additionally, traders can enhance liquidity by trading options that are closer to the money (ATM) or have shorter expiration periods, as these tend to be more liquid.

A cautionary tale from the trading floor involves a novice trader who launched an iron condor on a mid-cap stock two weeks before its earnings announcement. Seduced by the high implied volatility (and potential premium income), the trader overlooked the stock's mediocre options liquidity. When the stock made an unexpected move post-earnings, the trader found it arduous to adjust the position without incurring significant losses due to the wide bid-ask spreads.

Liquidity considerations are paramount in the architecture of iron condor strategies. They influence not just the potential profitability but also the flexibility and risk management capabilities of the strategy. By prioritizing liquidity in both the selection of underlying assets and options, traders can navigate the iron condor strategy with greater confidence and agility, aligning themselves with the currents of the market for optimal outcomes.

Volatility Characteristics

volatility represents the degree of variation in the price of an asset over time. It is the heartbeat of the market, a pulse that can quicken with fear or slow with complacency. For iron condor traders, volatility is a double-edged sword. On one hand, elevated volatility levels can inflate premiums, offering the tantalizing prospect of higher returns. On the other, increased volatility also augments risk, as the probability of an underlying asset breaching the iron condor's boundaries grows.

Understanding volatility necessitates a bifurcation into historical (realized) volatility and implied volatility. Historical volatility measures past price movements, providing a rearview mirror perspective on market dynamics. Conversely, implied volatility, embedded in option prices, reflects the market's forecast of future volatility. An iron condor strategist must be adept at reading both, using historical volatility to gauge trends and implied volatility to anticipate market sentiment.

Case Study: The Volatility Paradox

Consider the hypothetical stock of Globex Corporation, which has exhibited low historical volatility over the past year, moving within a narrow price range. An iron condor trader might view this as an ideal candidate, expecting the calm to persist. However, a looming product launch could spike implied volatility, as the market braces for potential price swings. This scenario encapsulates the volatility paradox: low historical volatility does not guarantee low implied volatility, and vice versa.

A critical concept in volatility characteristics is the volatility skew—a pattern that reveals options with lower strike prices (further out-of-the-money) often have higher implied volatility than those closer to the money. For iron condor traders, this skew can be a nemesis, as it suggests an asymmetric risk of significant price moves to the downside. Understanding and monitoring the volatility skew is paramount for adjusting the strike prices of the iron condor to mitigate this risk.

To leverage volatility in favor of the iron condor strategy, traders must develop a nuanced understanding of volatility cycles. Market events, earnings announcements, and macroeconomic reports can all influence volatility. Traders might employ a dynamic approach, initiating iron condor positions when implied volatility is high (and premiums are lush) and preferring caution when volatility is low. Additionally, the use of volatility analytics tools can provide a strategic edge, enabling traders to visualize potential volatility patterns and adjust their strategies accordingly.

A quintessential example of volatility in action is observed during earnings season. The anticipation of an earnings announcement can inflate a stock's implied volatility, as traders speculate on the outcome. For instance, an iron condor trader might analyze the historic volatility surges of PharmaTech Inc. around its earnings dates. By timing the establishment of iron condor positions to capitalize on the heightened implied volatility (and subsequent volatility crush post-announcement), the trader can optimize the strategy's profit potential.

Earnings and Event-Driven Strategy Adjustments

The period before an earnings announcement is fraught with speculation, leading to a palpable increase in implied volatility. Savvy traders understand that this is a double-edged sword. High implied volatility can inflate option premiums, presenting an attractive entry point for establishing new positions. However, the unpredictability of an earnings outcome necessitates a cautious approach.

Example: Let's consider the case of Quantum Innovations, a tech giant known for its groundbreaking products. Ahead of its Q2 earnings report, market analysts are divided, fostering an atmosphere ripe with speculative fervor. An iron condor trader, recognizing the volatility spike, might opt to adjust their strategy by narrowing the wings of their condor, thus reducing potential risk exposure while still capitalizing on the elevated premiums.

During the Event: Weathering the Storm

The unveiling of earnings is akin to a storm breaking upon the markets—swift and potentially devastating. Here, the iron condor trader's mettle is tested. The immediate aftermath of an earnings report can see dramatic price swings, often breaching the boundaries set by a previously stable iron condor.

Strategic agility is key during these moments. Consider the scenario involving EcoTech Renewables, a company at the forefront of sustainable energy. An unexpectedly positive earnings report sends its stock soaring. Traders with active iron condor positions now face the risk of the upper bounds being breached. A preemptive strategy involves closely monitoring the position during the announcement and being prepared to make swift adjustments, such as closing out the call spread to mitigate losses.

Post-Event: Navigating the Aftermath

Once the dust settles, the post-earnings landscape presents a new set of opportunities and challenges. Typically, implied volatility declines sharply after an announcement (known as the volatility crush), affecting the value of options positions.

In the wake of EcoTech's earnings report, while the initial surge might have jeopardized the iron condor, the subsequent volatility crush could render options less valuable, providing a chance to close positions at a reduced cost or even realign the strategy to reflect the new market conditions.

Event-Driven Strategy Adjustments Beyond Earnings

While earnings announcements are a primary focus, other

market events—such as product launches, regulatory approvals, or geopolitical shifts—also necessitate strategic adjustments. The iron condor trader must remain vigilant, adapting to the ever-changing market panorama.

Example: The announcement of a groundbreaking partnership between VirtualSpace Gaming and a major console manufacturer presents a similar volatility scenario to earnings reports. Traders might employ event-driven adjustments, anticipating the increased volatility and adjusting their iron condor spreads accordingly.

In the digital age, technology serves as the trader's compass. Leveraging sophisticated analytics tools allows for real-time monitoring and adjustment of positions based on volatility indices, news sentiment analysis, and market signals. These tools become invaluable, especially when navigating the precarious periods surrounding earnings and significant events.

Mastering earnings and event-driven strategy adjustments within the iron condor framework is an art form that combines keen market insight with the precision of timely decision-making. By understanding the dynamics at play and employing strategic adjustments, traders can protect their positions from undue risk and potentially harness the volatility for greater rewards. In the final analysis, the ability to adapt—not just predict—defines the successful iron condor strategist amidst the unpredictable ebb and flow of the options trading seas.

Determining Optimal Strike Prices and Expiration

The selection of strike prices and expiration dates forms the cornerstone of crafting an iron condor strategy that balances risk with reward, a strategic endeavor that requires a synthesis of market analysis, risk assessment, and personal trading objectives. This segment will dissect the multifaceted process of determining the optimal strike prices and expiration periods for iron condor trades, providing traders with a framework to enhance their strategic approach.

The Interplay of Strike Price Selection and Market Volatility

Choosing the right strike prices is akin to setting the sails for a journey across the volatile seas of the options market. It's about finding the sweet spot where the trade can withstand the market's unpredictable gusts without capsizing.

Example: Consider a scenario where MacroTech, a leading semiconductor company, is experiencing heightened volatility due to supply chain uncertainties. An iron condor trader might select strike prices that are further out-of-the-money (OTM) for both the call and put spreads, accounting for the expected price swings and aiming to maintain the position within the profit range.

Leveraging Expiration Times to Capitalize on Time Decay

The time until expiration of the options in an iron condor is a crucial factor that can significantly impact the position's profitability. Theta, or time decay, benefits the iron condor strategy since the value of the options sold (the call and put spreads) decreases over time, ceteris paribus.

In the MacroTech scenario, choosing an expiration 30 to 60 days out might strike a balance between capitalizing on time decay and allowing enough time to manage the position if the market moves unfavorably. This timeframe provides a window where the theta decay accelerates, enhancing the potential profitability of the iron condor while also offering a buffer period for adjustments.

The Role of Implied Volatility in Strike and Expiration Selection

Implied volatility (IV) is a projection of a stock's future volatility and plays a pivotal role in options pricing. An astute trader must scrutinize IV levels when selecting strike prices and expiration dates to optimize an iron condor setup.

Utilizing the IV Rank or IV Percentile can guide the trader in understanding whether the current IV is high or low relative to its historical values. In periods of high IV, traders might opt for wider spreads between the strike prices to account for larger expected market moves while also benefiting from higher premiums collected.

Example: If MacroTech's IV Rank is unusually high due to the looming supply chain announcement, a trader might choose strike prices that are further apart, effectively creating a wider iron condor. This adjustment aims to safeguard the position against significant price swings while taking advantage of the elevated premiums. The selected expiration should then align with the period post-announcement, when a decrease in IV (volatility crush) is anticipated, potentially enhancing the profitability of the iron condor through premium decay.

Dynamic Adjustments: The Key to Adapting Strike Prices and Expiration

The markets are an ever-changing environment, and flexibility is paramount. Continuous monitoring and potential adjustments of strike prices and expiration dates are integral to managing risk and capitalizing on opportunities.

For instance, should MacroTech's stock begin to trend strongly in one direction as the supply chain issues resolve, the trader may need to adjust the position by rolling the threatened side of the condor to different strike prices or a later expiration, thereby managing risk and seeking to preserve the trade's profitability.

In today's trading landscape, the use of sophisticated tools and models, such as the Black-Scholes model for pricing options or Monte Carlo simulations for forecasting price movements, can provide traders with a competitive edge in determining optimal strike prices and expirations. These tools offer a data-driven basis for decisions, reducing reliance on gut feeling and enhancing the strategic depth of iron condor trading.

Determining the optimal strike prices and expiration dates for an iron condor is a balancing act of risk and reward, requiring a nuanced understanding of market dynamics, volatility, and the mechanics of option pricing. Through careful analysis, strategic planning, and the willingness to adjust as conditions change, traders can navigate the complexities of the options market, aiming for a strategic position that meets their risk tolerance and trading objectives. In this endeavor, technology and quantitative models serve as invaluable allies, providing insights and foresight in the ever-evolving world of options trading.

Delta as a Guide for Strike Selection

Delta, in the context of options trading, measures the sensitivity of an option's price to a $1 change in the price of the underlying asset. Represented as a number between -1 and 1 for puts and 0 to 1 for calls, delta not only provides insights into the option's price movement correlation with the underlying but also offers a probabilistic forecast of the option ending in-the-money (ITM).

Example: For a call option on QuantumScape, a company pioneering in solid-state battery technology, with a delta of 0, this implies that for every $1 increase in QuantumScape's stock, the price of the call option is expected to rise by $30, assuming all other factors remain constant.

Delta in Strike Selection: Balancing Precision and Protection

In constructing an iron condor, selecting strikes with an appropriate delta is crucial. The goal is to identify OTM options that have a balanced probability of expiring worthless, thereby allowing the trader to retain the premium collected at the trade's inception. A common practice is to target options with a delta ranging from to 0, balancing the dual objectives of premium collection and risk mitigation.

Applying Delta: A Real-World Scenario

Consider Helios Energy, an emerging player in renewable energy, exhibiting moderate volatility. For an iron condor strategy, a trader might look at selling a put option with a delta of -5, signaling a 25% theoretical probability of the option expiring ITM, and simultaneously selling a call option with a delta of 5. This approach aims to position the iron condor's wings safely OTM, thereby maximizing the chance of the options expiring worthless and the trader pocketing the premiums.

Delta is not static; it evolves with the market. In a scenario where Helios Energy announces a breakthrough in solar panel efficiency, causing increased stock volatility, the deltas of existing positions may shift. A diligent trader monitors these deltas, ready to make strategic adjustments. For instance, if the call option's delta escalates beyond the initial threshold, rolling the call to a higher strike with a lower delta may be prudent, rebalancing the iron condor to align with the new market dynamics.

While delta is instrumental in strike selection, its efficacy is magnified when used in conjunction with other Greeks such as gamma, theta, and vega. Gamma measures the rate of change of delta, providing insight into delta's stability. Theta quantifies time decay, a critical element in the iron condor strategy, while vega assesses sensitivity to volatility. A holistic view, considering all Greeks, empowers traders to fine-tune their iron condors to the nuanced fabric of market conditions and volatility landscapes.

Example: In adjusting the Helios Energy iron condor amidst shifting market sentiment, a trader evaluates not only the deltas but also the theta to ensure the positions benefit from accelerated time decay as expiration nears, and vega, to understand how impending volatility might impact the options' premiums.

Delta serves as a critical guide in the selection of strike prices for the iron condor strategy, offering a pathway through the complexities of options trading. By understanding and applying delta judiciously, traders can navigate the turbulent markets with informed precision, optimizing their iron condor setups for a blend of resilience and profitability. This strategic utilization of delta underscores its role not merely as a metric but as a cornerstone in the architecture of sophisticated trading strategies, enabling traders to harness the options market with confidence and strategic acumen.

Theta Decay and Time to Expiration

Theta represents the rate at which an option's value diminishes as it approaches its expiration date, with all other factors held constant. This relentless erosion of value is an intrinsic feature of options, reflecting the decreasing window for the option to end in-the-money (ITM).

Example: Imagine an option on the Vanguard Total Stock Market ETF (VTI), a proxy for the broader market, with a theta of -0.05. This indicates that with each passing day, the option's price is expected to decrease by 5 cents under a ceteris paribus condition.

Strategic Implications for Iron Condors

The iron condor strategy, a favorite among traders for its potential to generate income through premium collection, is particularly sensitive to theta decay. Given that the strategy entails selling out-of-the-money (OTM) call and put options, the acceleration of theta decay as expiration nears serves as a crucial ally. The strategy's success hinges not on significant moves in the underlying asset, but rather on the options expiring worthless, allowing the trader to retain the full premium.

Consider Icarus Aerospace, a company in the midst of a technological breakthrough, thus attracting considerable attention from options traders. In establishing an iron condor on Icarus Aerospace, a trader opts for options with 45 days until expiration, aiming to balance the potential premium against the risk posed by time decay.

As days pass, the theta decay intensifies, gradually eroding the value of the options sold. Assuming relatively stable prices for Icarus Aerospace stock, the trader observes the value of the sold options decline, inching closer to the optimal outcome—expiration worthless.

The interplay between theta decay and market movements necessitates vigilance and adaptability. Amidst heightened volatility, an unexpected surge in Icarus Aerospace's stock might diminish the likelihood of the call options expiring worthless. Here, the trader must assess whether adjusting the position—perhaps by rolling the call options to a higher strike price with a later expiration—could realign the strategy with the altered market landscape.

Beyond its direct implications, theta decay influences the strategic calculus through its interaction with other Greeks, such as delta and vega. For instance, a rise in volatility (vega) might increase an option's value, counteracting the effect of theta decay. In crafting an iron condor, understanding and anticipating these dynamics enables traders to tailor their strategies, selecting strikes and expirations that offer a favorable convergence of decay rate and market volatility.

Example: Returning to the Icarus Aerospace scenario, the trader monitors not only the theta decay but also the delta for signs of increasing in-the-money probability and vega for volatility-induced price changes. This holistic approach ensures that decisions are informed by a comprehensive view of the market forces at play.

Theta decay, a constant yet variable force, underscores the temporal nature of options trading. In the context of the iron condor strategy, its mastery is tantamount to harnessing time itself—transforming what is often viewed as an adversary into a strategic ally. Through careful selection of expiration dates and vigilant management of positions against the backdrop of market dynamics, traders can optimize the impact of theta decay, navigating the options market with precision and poise. This dance with time, when executed with skill, elevates the iron condor strategy from mere theory to a potent instrument in the trader's arsenal, offering a pathway to potential profitability through the measured exploitation of time's inexorable march.

Balancing Risk vs. Reward

The iron condor strategy is a testament to the balance of risk and reward. By selling an out-of-the-money call spread and a put spread simultaneously, the trader creates a position that profits from a range-bound market. However, the finite bounds of profit and loss zones necessitate a nuanced understanding of risk management.

Example: Consider a scenario involving Helios Energy, a company emblematic of the volatile energy sector. A trader might construct an iron condor around Helios by selecting strikes for the call and put spreads that align with historical volatility patterns, seeking to maximize premium income while managing potential losses.

Risk Management Tactics

Effective risk management within the iron condor strategy involves several key considerations:

- Selection of Strike Prices: The choice of strike prices directly impacts the risk-reward profile of the trade. Strikes closer to the current price of the underlying increase potential reward but also risk, as the probability of the options being exercised rises.

- Position Sizing: Proper position sizing is crucial. Even the most well-constructed iron condor can face losses, and it is essential to ensure that no single trade can significantly impact the overall portfolio.

- Adjustments: Active management and the willingness to adjust open positions can mitigate risk. For example, if Helios Energy unexpectedly breaks out of its range, adjusting or closing the position can cap losses.

Reward Optimization Techniques

While risk management focuses on minimizing potential losses, optimizing reward involves maximizing the income potential of the trade:

- Exploitation of Volatility: High volatility increases option premiums, presenting an opportunity to enter iron condor positions with higher potential returns. However, this comes with increased risk, as the wider price swings can breach the strike boundaries.

- Timing: Entry and exit timing can significantly affect the profitability of iron condors. Entering when premiums are high and exiting as theta decay accelerates can enhance returns.

A Practical Application: Balancing Act in Real-Time

Let's apply these concepts to a real-time market scenario with Helios Energy. Given its historical volatility, a trader might opt for an iron condor that captures a higher premium while maintaining a manageable risk profile. By carefully selecting strike prices that are a standard deviation away from Helios's current price, the trader crafts a position that balances the potential for profit with the risk of loss.

As the trade progresses, Helios Energy's stock exhibits unexpected volatility due to geopolitical tensions affecting energy prices. The trader, monitoring the situation closely, decides to adjust the call spread of the iron condor, moving the strikes higher to avoid potential loss. This adjustment reflects a dynamic response to the unfolding market conditions, demonstrating the critical importance of flexibility in balancing risk and reward.

Balancing risk and reward in the context of the iron condor strategy is an art form that requires knowledge, intuition, and discipline. By comprehensively understanding the mechanics of the strategy and applying the principles of risk management and reward optimization, traders can navigate the complexities of the options market. Through calculated strike selection, vigilant position sizing, and strategic adjustments, the pursuit of equilibrium becomes a disciplined approach to trading, where the scales of risk and reward are meticulously managed to achieve trading objectives.

Executing the Trade

Prior to executing an iron condor trade, a comprehensive pre-execution checklist is paramount. This checklist ensures that all relevant factors have been considered, laying a foundation for informed decision-making.

- Market Analysis: A thorough analysis of the market conditions and the specific underlying asset is crucial. For instance, a trader considering an iron condor on the S&P 500 index would assess current market volatility, historical performance, and upcoming economic indicators.

- Selection of Underlying Asset: The choice of the underlying asset is influenced by its liquidity, volatility, and the trader's familiarity with the asset. High liquidity ensures tighter bid-ask spreads, which is vital for minimizing execution costs.

- Strike Price and Expiry Date Determination: Based on the market analysis and volatility assessment, strike prices for the call and put spreads are chosen to optimize the risk-reward ratio. The expiry date is selected to balance the time decay (theta) and the trader's outlook on the underlying asset.

The Mechanics of Trade Execution

Executing an iron condor involves placing four separate but related orders: selling an out-of-the-money (OTM) call, buying an OTM call with a higher strike price, selling an OTM put, and buying an OTM put with a lower strike price. This creates a defined-risk, defined-reward scenario.

Example: Let us consider executing an iron condor on XYZ Corporation, which is currently trading at $100. Based on our analysis, we decide to structure our iron condor around the following options:

- Sell a call option with a strike price of $110 (OTM) and buy a call option with a strike price of $115 (OTM) to cap the maximum loss on the upside.

- Sell a put option with a strike price of $90 (OTM) and buy a put option with a strike price of $85 (OTM) to limit the downside risk.

Execution Platforms and Order Types

Choosing the right trading platform and understanding the order types is critical for executing the iron condor efficiently. Most platforms will allow the trade to be executed as a single order, which simplifies the process and helps maintain the desired risk-reward profile.

- Limit Orders vs. Market Orders: For executing iron condors, limit orders are often preferred as they allow the trader to specify the maximum acceptable premium for the iron condor, providing control over the entry price.

- Monitoring for Execution: Once the order is placed, it is essential to monitor the market and the order status. If the market moves significantly, it may be necessary to adjust the limit price to achieve execution.

Post-Execution Considerations

After successfully entering the trade, the focus shifts to management and potential adjustment strategies. Monitoring the underlying asset and being prepared to make adjustments based on market movements are critical aspects of managing an iron condor.

Example Continued: In the case of XYZ Corporation, suppose after executing the iron condor, the stock experiences unexpected volatility due to a merger announcement. The trader needs to be ready to adjust the position, potentially by closing out the threatened side of the iron condor to limit losses or lock in profits.

The execution of the iron condor strategy encapsulates the transition from theory to practice, embodying the synthesis of analytical preparation and operational precision. Successful execution hinges on a robust pre-execution checklist, a clear understanding of the mechanics involved, and the adept use of execution platforms. By mastering these elements, traders can navigate the complexities of the market with confidence, transforming strategic insights into profitable outcomes. The narrative of executing the trade is not merely about placing orders; it's about orchestrating a symphony of decisions that balance risk, reward, and reality in the quest for trading excellence.

Order Types and Placement Strategy

The choice of order type is a pivotal element in the execution of any trading strategy, especially for complex setups like the iron condor. Here, we explore the most commonly employed order types in the context of options trading and how they apply to the iron condor strategy.

- Limit Orders: A limit order allows the trader to specify a price limit—the maximum price they are willing to pay when buying an option or the minimum they are willing to accept when selling. For iron condors, limit orders are indispensable, enabling traders to control the entry cost and, consequently, the risk-reward ratio of the strategy.

- Market Orders: While market orders ensure immediate execution, they leave traders at the mercy of the current market price, which can be particularly precarious in the fast-moving options market. Given the precision required in setting up an iron condor, market orders are less favored due to their lack of price control.

- Stop-Loss Orders: Although not directly used in the initial setup of an iron condor, stop-loss orders play a crucial role in risk management. By setting a stop-loss order, traders can specify a point at which a losing position is automatically closed, thus capping potential losses.

- Conditional Orders: These orders are executed only when specific conditions are met. In the context of iron condors, conditional orders can be strategically used to enter the trade when the underlying asset reaches a particular price level or volatility index.

Crafting the Placement Strategy

With an understanding of the different order types, we turn

our attention to the strategic placement of these orders. The objective is to enter the iron condor position with an optimal balance of risk, reward, and probability of success.

- Pinpointing the Entry Point: Utilizing technical analysis, market trends, and volatility indicators, traders can identify potential entry points where the underlying asset's price and market conditions align with the strategy's requirements. For example, entering an iron condor during periods of high volatility can result in higher premiums received, enhancing the strategy's profitability potential.

- Setting the Limit Price: The limit price for the iron condor should be determined by evaluating the premium's current market rates, desired risk-reward balance, and the trader's outlook on the underlying asset. A carefully chosen limit price maximizes the chance of order execution while ensuring the trade aligns with the trader's risk tolerance and objectives.

- Timing the Market: While timing the market perfectly is an elusive goal, certain times of the trading day exhibit less volatility, potentially offering more stable entry points for the iron condor setup. For instance, avoiding the market open and close times can mitigate the impact of sudden price swings on the execution of limit orders.

Example: Consider a trader preparing to enter an iron condor on the S&P 500 ETF (SPY). After comprehensive analysis, they decide the optimal conditions are met when SPY is trading around $330. They set a limit order for the entire iron condor setup with a net premium that aligns with their risk-reward criteria. By choosing a mid-day timeframe for order placement, the trader aims to benefit from reduced market volatility, enhancing the likelihood of order execution at the desired price.

The Art of Strategic Execution

The meticulous selection and strategic placement of orders are fundamental to the successful execution of the iron condor strategy. By mastering the nuances of order types and developing a coherent placement strategy, traders can navigate the complexities of the options market with greater precision. This approach not only optimizes the entry and management of the iron condor but also underscores the importance of adaptability and strategic planning in the pursuit of trading proficiency. the careful orchestration of order types and placement strategy is a critical step in transforming theoretical knowledge into practical trading success.

Monitoring the Position Post-Execution

Effective post-execution monitoring hinges on several core pillars, each contributing to the trader's ability to respond proactively to market dynamics.

- Real-Time Data Analysis: Staying abreast of real-time market data is crucial. Utilizing trading platforms that offer live quotes, charts, and analytics tools enables traders to observe the immediate impact of market movements on their positions.

- Key Performance Indicators (KPIs): Identifying specific KPIs such as delta, gamma, theta, and vega helps traders understand their position's sensitivity to various market factors. These Greeks offer insights into how changes in the market price, time decay, and volatility could affect the iron condor's performance.

- Setting Alerts: Modern trading platforms allow traders to

set customizable alerts based on price movements, volatility changes, or other relevant factors. These alerts serve as an early warning system, enabling traders to take timely actions without the need to constantly monitor their screens.

Strategic Adjustment Considerations

Monitoring is not just about observation; it's about being prepared to adjust the iron condor strategy in response to market changes.

- Identifying Adjustment Triggers: Before entering the trade, outline specific scenarios or thresholds that would trigger an adjustment. These might include a significant shift in the underlying asset's price, reaching a specific profit or loss level, or changes in implied volatility.

- Adjustment Strategies: Common adjustments include rolling out to a further expiration date, tightening or widening the spreads, or closing out one side of the iron condor to reduce exposure. Each adjustment carries its own risks and opportunities, requiring a balanced assessment of the current situation.

Example: Imagine a trader has an iron condor set on the NASDAQ 100 index. They receive an alert that the upper bound of their condor is nearing the current market price due to an unexpected tech rally. The trader reviews the position's delta and decides to roll up the put side to reduce delta exposure and balance the position, thereby managing risk while keeping the trade active.

Emotional Discipline and Decision Making

Beyond the technical aspects, effective monitoring is deeply intertwined with emotional discipline. The stress of potential losses or the greed of early profits can cloud judgment.

- Adhering to the Trading Plan: A well-defined trading plan includes criteria for monitoring and adjustment. Sticking to this plan helps traders make decisions based on strategy rather than emotion.

- Reflective Practice: Taking notes on decisions made during the monitoring phase and reflecting on those decisions after the trade concludes. This practice aids in refining the monitoring strategy over time, learning from both successes and setbacks.

Mastering the Art of Vigilance

The post-execution phase of the iron condor strategy is as critical as the initial setup. By embracing the principles of real-time data analysis, strategic adjustment, and emotional discipline, traders can enhance their ability to steer through the unpredictable seas of the options market. Monitoring with vigilance and readiness to adapt ensures that traders not only safeguard their positions but also capitalize on opportunities to optimize performance, ultimately mastering the art of iron condor trading.

Through diligent oversight, strategic adjustments, and an unwavering commitment to their trading blueprint, traders transform the challenge of monitoring into an opportunity for growth, learning, and profit.

Dealing with Assignment Risk

Assignment risk occurs when the holder of an option decides to exercise their right to buy (in the case of call options) or sell (in the case of put options) the underlying asset. For iron condor traders, this risk is most pertinent when the market price of the underlying asset moves close to or beyond the strike prices of the sold options.

- Scenario Example: Consider an iron condor placed on Company X's stock, with short call options at a strike price of $105 and short put options at a strike price of $95. If Company X's stock soars beyond $105 as the expiration date approaches, the call options are increasingly at risk of being assigned.

Mitigation Strategies

Mitigation of assignment risk begins with strategic selection and continuous monitoring of the iron condor's components.

- Choosing European-style Options: One straightforward approach is to use European-style options, which can only be exercised at expiration, not before.

- Close Monitoring of In-The-Money Options: Keeping a vigilant eye on options that move in-the-money as they are more likely to be assigned. Traders should consider closing or rolling these options to reduce risk.

- Setting Alerts: Utilize trading platform alerts for significant price movements or when options move in-the-money, allowing for timely decision-making.

Preventive Measures

The best defense against assignment risk is a good offense in the form of preventive measures taken at the onset and during the life of the iron condor trade.

- Spread Width and Expiration Selection: Opt for spreads that are wide enough to provide a buffer against moderate price movements but not so wide that they significantly reduce the trade's profitability. Similarly, choosing expiration dates that align with the trader's market outlook and risk tolerance can help mitigate assignment risk.

- Timely Adjustments: If an option moves in-the-money, traders might consider rolling the option to a further expiration date or adjusting the strike price. This maneuver requires balancing the cost of the adjustment against the potential risk of assignment.

Handling Assignment

Even with the best preventive measures, assignment can still occur. The manner in which a trader responds can markedly affect the outcome.

- Immediate Assessment: Upon assignment, assess the overall position immediately to understand the impact on the iron condor strategy. The assigned leg might expose the trader to significant market risk or, conversely, provide an opportunity to close the position at a favorable price.

- Executing a Response: If the stock of Company X is assigned via the short call options, the trader might need to deliver the stock. If they do not own the underlying stock, they will have to purchase it at the current market price, potentially at a loss. Conversely, if put options are assigned, the trader will have to purchase the underlying asset at the strike price, which could be higher than the market price.

- Post-Assignment Strategy: After addressing the immediate implications of assignment, revisit the iron condor strategy to adjust the remaining positions accordingly. This might involve closing out the trade to prevent further losses or adjusting the remaining legs to salvage or even enhance the trade's profitability.

Transforming Risk into Opportunity

Dealing with assignment risk is an integral aspect of trading iron condors, demanding a blend of proactive strategy and reactive agility. By understanding the mechanics of assignment, employing mitigation strategies, and effectively handling any assignments that occur, traders can transform potential risks into opportunities for refinement and growth within their trading approach.

Through careful planning, vigilant monitoring, and strategic adjustments, traders can navigate the complexities of assignment risk, ensuring that their iron condor positions are managed with precision and foresight.

Leveraging Market Conditions

Volatility, the double-edged sword of the trading world, presents both peril and promise. Understanding its dual nature is crucial for traders looking to leverage market conditions effectively.

- High Volatility Strategies: In a high volatility environment, the premiums on options can be significantly higher, presenting an attractive opportunity for iron condor traders. However, the increased risk of price movements breaching the condor's wings requires strategic adjustments. Traders can consider narrowing the spread between the strike prices of their options to reduce risk, albeit at the cost of potential profit margins.

- Example: During the earnings season, a company expected to report significant news may experience heightened volatility. An iron condor strategy in such a scenario might involve closer strike prices to protect against sudden large movements in the stock price.

- Low Volatility Approaches: Conversely, in periods of low volatility, options premiums are lower, suggesting a different tactic. Traders may opt for wider spreads between their strike prices, increasing the potential profit margin while accepting the lower likelihood of price movements that could threaten their positions.

- Example: In a stable market phase, with Company Y's stock showing minimal fluctuations, a trader might place an iron condor with strike prices far apart, capitalizing on the predictability of the market's movements.

Trend Utilization in Iron Condor Trading

Beyond volatility, discerning the trend or direction of the market is critical for adjusting iron condor strategies effectively.

- Bullish or Bearish Adjustments: If the market shows a clear direction, iron condor traders can skew their positions to favor the anticipated movement. For example, in a bullish trend, traders might position their call spreads closer to the money than their put spreads, tilting the risk/reward profile in favor of the expected rise.

- Strategic Example: Anticipating a gradual uptrend in the S&P 500 index, a trader adjusts their iron condor to have puts with lower deltas and calls that are nearer to the money, thus slightly biasing the position towards benefiting from the uptrend while still maintaining a fundamentally neutral stance.

Seasonal and Event-Driven Adjustments

Certain times of the year or specific events can drastically alter market conditions, providing astute traders with the chance to adjust their iron condor strategies accordingly.

- Seasonal Fluctuations: Historical trends show that some markets exhibit seasonal patterns, such as the end-of-year rally in stock markets. Traders can adjust their iron condor setups in anticipation of these patterns, positioning themselves to capitalize on predictable movements.

- Event-Driven Strategies: Major events, such as elections, product launches, or regulatory changes, can lead to significant market reactions. Iron condor traders should stay informed and ready to adjust their positions based on their analysis of the event's potential impacts.

- Real-World Application: In the lead-up to a crucial Federal

Reserve announcement regarding interest rates, a trader might adjust their iron condor positions, expecting increased market volatility. The adjustments could involve tightening the spreads or shifting the center of the condor to better align with anticipated market movements.

CHAPTER 4:
LEVERAGING MARKET
CONDITIONS

I n options trading, high volatility environments are both a siren and a beacon to the astute trader. These periods, characterized by rapid and significant price movements within financial markets, present a double-edged sword: the promise of higher profits and the peril of increased risk. Navigating these tumultuous waters requires a blend of strategic foresight, disciplined risk management, and an in-depth understanding of volatility's multifaceted impact on options strategies.

To comprehend how high volatility environments affect options trading, one must first grasp what volatility signifies in the financial lexicon. Volatility measures the rate at which the price of a security increases or decreases for a given set of returns. In options trading, volatility is paramount because it directly influences option premiums. The higher the volatility, the greater the price movement a stock is expected to have, and consequently, the higher the premium an options trader can command for selling the option.

The iron condor, a strategy designed to profit from a stock trading in a narrow range, faces unique challenges and opportunities in high volatility environments. The essence of the iron condor lies in its structure, which involves selling an out-of-the-money (OTM) put spread and an OTM call spread on the same underlying asset with the same expiration date. This structure is engineered to maximize the profit from the premium received if the asset price stays within a defined range.

High Volatility Strategies

1. Adjusting Strike Prices: In high volatility environments, the trader may opt to adjust the strike prices of both the call and put spreads further out-of-the-money. This adjustment aims to increase the probability of the underlying asset remaining within the strike prices, albeit at the cost of receiving a smaller premium.

2. Widening the Wings: Another approach involves widening the distance between the strike prices of the put and call spreads, known as 'the wings' of the condor. This strategy offers the dual benefits of increasing the range within which the underlying asset can fluctuate while still allowing the trader to retain the premium, and providing a cushion against the increased risk of price movements breaching the strike prices.

3. Active Management and Adjustment: High volatility necessitates a more hands-on approach to managing iron condor positions. Traders may need to closely monitor market movements and be prepared to make adjustments to their positions. This could involve rolling out positions to later expiration dates or adjusting the strike prices of the spreads to respond to market movements.

Risk Management

Effective risk management is the linchpin of success in high volatility environments. Traders must be vigilant in setting stop-loss orders to mitigate losses if the market moves unfavorably. Additionally, maintaining a balanced portfolio and employing diversification strategies can help spread risk, ensuring that a downturn in one position doesn't disproportionately affect the trader's overall portfolio.

The psychological aspect of trading in high volatility environments cannot be understated. The heightened tension and rapid pace of change can lead to impulsive decisions driven by fear or greed. Cultivating emotional discipline and adhering to a well-thought-out trading plan are critical to navigating these periods successfully.

Trading in high volatility environments presents a unique set of challenges and opportunities for the iron condor strategist. By understanding the dynamics of volatility and employing strategic adjustments, risk management, and psychological resilience, traders can harness the potential of these environments for substantial gains. However, the path is fraught with risk, and only those with the skill, discipline, and insight to navigate these stormy seas will emerge victorious.

The Impact on Premiums

The premium of an option is the price paid by the buyer to the seller, granting the buyer the right, but not the obligation, to buy (call option) or sell (put option) the underlying asset at a specified price (strike price) before the option expires.

The premium is not static but a dynamic entity, fluctuating in response to various market forces, with volatility being a principal driver.

High volatility signifies greater uncertainty in the market, implying larger potential price swings of the underlying asset within a short period. From the perspective of the seller (writer) of an option, this increased uncertainty augments the risk of the option being exercised, necessitating a higher premium to compensate for this elevated risk. Consequently, in high volatility environments, option premiums escalate, reflecting the amplified risk and potential reward scenario.

Implications for the Iron Condor Strategy

For traders employing the iron condor strategy, these inflationary premium conditions offer a seductive allure. The strategy's initial setup, involving the sale of out-of-the-money put and call spreads, garners its profit from the premiums received. High volatility, by inflating these premiums, seemingly promises richer rewards. However, this is a double-edged sword.

1. Increased Profit Potential: The immediate benefit of high volatility is the increased premium that can be collected. This elevates the potential profit for iron condor setups, as the strategy profits from the premiums retained when the option contracts expire worthless.

2. Enhanced Risk: While the prospect of higher premiums is attractive, it comes with the contingent of enhanced risk. The wider price swings increase the likelihood of the underlying asset breaching the boundaries set by the strike prices of the iron

condor, potentially leading to losses.

Strategic Adjustments

In light of these dynamics, iron condor traders might consider several strategic adjustments:

- Premium Monitoring: Closely monitor the premiums of potential iron condor setups, identifying those that offer a favorable balance between high premium income and manageable risk.

- Selective Trading: Adopt a more selective approach to initiating iron condor trades. High volatility might increase premiums across the board, but not all opportunities will be worth the risk. Focus on underlying assets with a history of reverting to mean prices or those less susceptible to extreme market movements.

- Hedging: Consider employing hedging strategies to mitigate risk. This could involve setting aside a portion of the increased premium income to purchase protective options that will pay off if the market moves against the iron condor position.

The impact of high volatility on premiums presents a nuanced challenge for iron condor traders. While it augurs the potential for increased profits through higher premiums, it simultaneously elevates the risk of adverse price movements. Through a combination of strategic adjustments, risk management, and a disciplined approach to trading, traders can navigate these turbulent premium waters, capitalizing on opportunities while safeguarding against the perils inherent in high volatility environments.

Adjusting Strike Widths and Positions

The iron condor, lie two pairs of options: one call spread and one put spread. Each spread consists of options with different strike prices. The difference between these strike prices within a spread is known as the "strike width." This parameter is not merely a technical detail; it is a critical factor that directly influences the potential profit and risk associated with the trade.

Strategic Implications of Adjusting Strike Widths

1. Risk Management: Increasing the strike width can potentially lead to higher profits since the premium received is generally higher for spreads with larger differences between strike prices. However, this comes at the cost of increased risk, as the trader is now more exposed to the possibility of the underlying asset's price moving beyond the outer strikes of the condor.

2. Profit Maximization: Conversely, narrowing the strike width reduces the maximum potential profit but also limits the trader's risk. This adjustment is particularly pertinent in high volatility environments where price swings can be more pronounced, and the probability of breaching the iron condor's boundaries is higher.

The Dynamics of Position Adjustments

Adjusting positions within the iron condor framework refers to the strategic realignment of the strike prices of the call and put spreads in anticipation of or in reaction to market movements. This maneuver is instrumental in tailoring the iron condor's exposure to the underlying asset's price action.

Tactical Considerations for Position Adjustments

- Anticipating Market Movements: In a market anticipated to shift direction, adjusting the position of the strike prices can align the iron condor more favorably with the expected movement. For instance, if a slight bullish shift is anticipated, shifting the call spread slightly outwards (upwards in strike price) while adjusting the put spread inwards (downwards in strike price) can optimize the position for profit.

- Responding to Volatility Changes: In periods of increasing volatility, traders might opt to position their strikes further from the current price of the underlying asset to accommodate wider price fluctuations, thereby reducing the likelihood of breaching the iron condor's boundaries.

Execution with Precision

- Market Analysis: Successful adjustments require a deep understanding of market indicators, sentiment, and potential triggers for volatility. This analysis forms the basis for strategic decisions on strike widths and positions.

- Timing: The timing of adjustments is crucial. Too early, and the trader may miss out on premium income; too late, and the market may have already moved unfavorably. The optimal timing hinges on a careful balance between market signals and the iron condor's expiration.

- Risk Assessment: Each adjustment carries its own set of risks and rewards. Traders must continually assess their positions, considering the potential impacts of their adjustments on the overall risk profile of their iron condor setup.

The strategic adjustments of strike widths and positions within the iron condor strategy are not mere tactical tweaks but foundational elements in the crafting of a successful trade. These adjustments, made with a keen understanding of market dynamics and a clear assessment of risk tolerance, allow traders to navigate the complex landscapes of options trading with agility and foresight, optimizing their positions for profitability while managing the inherent risks. Through meticulous planning and execution, traders can leverage these adjustments to align their strategies with the prevailing market conditions, turning volatility and uncertainty into opportunities for strategic gain.

Protective Measures Against Swift Market Moves

In the unforgiving arena of options trading, where fortunes can pivot on the whims of market sentiment, protective measures against swift market moves are not merely a strategy but an imperative. This discourse explores the arsenal of tactics that traders wield to shield their positions from the sudden gusts of volatility, focusing on the preservation of capital in the iron condor strategy amidst unpredictably swift market moves.

Swift market moves are typically triggered by unforeseen events or significant economic announcements. These can include geopolitical developments, corporate earnings reports surpassing or falling short of expectations, or sudden shifts in governmental policies. The repercussions of these events ripple through the markets, often resulting in abrupt price changes that can endanger exposed options positions.

To navigate these turbulent waters, traders employ various strategies designed to protect their positions from the potential havoc wrought by rapid market movements.

1. Use of Stop-Loss Orders: A fundamental protective measure is the implementation of stop-loss orders. These orders automatically close out positions once the asset reaches a predetermined price level, thus capping potential losses. For iron condor traders, stop-loss orders can be set for individual legs of the strategy, ensuring that a swift move against one part of the condor doesn't lead to disproportionate losses.

2. Position Sizing: Prudent position sizing is crucial in managing risk. By limiting the size of each iron condor relative to their overall portfolio, traders can ensure that a sudden adverse move doesn't disproportionately affect their capital. This strategy involves calculating the maximum potential loss for each iron condor and ensuring it does not exceed a specific percentage of the portfolio.

3. Hedging with Index Options: Another technique involves hedging iron condor positions with index options. For instance, if a trader has multiple iron condor positions that are vulnerable to a market downturn, purchasing put options on a major index like the S&P 500 can provide broad market protection. These index options increase in value during a market downturn, offsetting losses from the iron condor positions.

4. Adjusting Strikes Proactively: In anticipation of events known to cause market turbulence, such as earnings announcements or economic data releases, traders can proactively adjust the strike prices of their iron condor's spreads. Moving strikes further out of the money can reduce the likelihood of the underlying asset

breaching the condor's bounds, albeit at the cost of receiving a lower premium.

5. Time Decay (Theta) Management: Since the value of options decays over time, entering trades where this time decay works in the trader's favor is a subtle protective strategy. By establishing iron condors with a shorter duration until expiry, traders can benefit from rapid theta decay, which reduces the window of opportunity for swift market moves to impact the positions adversely.

The Importance of Continuous Monitoring and Adaptation

Protection against swift market moves is not a set-it-and-forget-it affair; it demands vigilance and the readiness to adapt. Continuous monitoring of market news, sentiment, and economic indicators is vital, allowing traders to anticipate potential triggers for volatility and take preemptive action. Moreover, a willingness to adjust strategies in response to evolving market conditions is crucial for preserving capital and achieving success in the dynamic world of options trading.

The specter of swift market moves looms large over the options trader, presenting challenges that demand respect, preparation, and strategic foresight. By employing a multifaceted approach to risk management—encompassing stop-loss orders, careful position sizing, hedging strategies, proactive adjustments, and adept timing—traders can fortify their iron condor positions against unexpected volatility. In doing so, they navigate the market's capricious tides with a measure of control, turning potential threats into opportunities for strategic refinement and growth.

Low volatility periods are characterized by smaller price movements in the underlying asset, creating a seemingly tranquil trading environment. However, this tranquility can often be misleading, as the reduced premium income from options selling strategies, such as iron condors, demands meticulous planning and execution to sustain profitability.

Adapting the Iron Condor in Low Volatility

1. Tightening the Spreads: In a low volatility environment, one approach is to tighten the wings of the iron condor—bringing the strike prices of the sold options closer to the current price of the underlying asset. This adjustment aims to increase the premium received, compensating for the lower volatility. However, this tactic also increases the risk of the underlying asset breaching the boundaries of the iron condor, necessitating vigilant risk management.

2. Choosing Shorter Expirations: Opting for iron condors with shorter expiration periods can be advantageous in low volatility settings. Shorter expirations capitalize on the rapid theta decay, allowing traders to benefit from time value erosion more swiftly. This strategy requires a fine balance, as shorter expirations also diminish the window for managing and adjusting the position if the market begins to move unfavorably.

3. Selective Underlying Selection: The choice of the underlying asset becomes paramount in low volatility scenarios. Traders might lean towards securities or indexes that, despite the broader market's calm, possess inherent volatility due to sector-specific factors or upcoming events. This selective approach aims to capture higher premiums without deviating significantly from the core principles of the iron condor

strategy.

4. Incremental Adjustments and Scaling: Adopting a gradual approach to position size and adjustments can serve traders well under low volatility. Instead of committing fully to a position from the outset, scaling in—gradually adding to the iron condor as the market validates the initial hypothesis—allows for a more flexible response to unexpected market shifts. Similarly, incremental adjustments to the strikes or the overall size of the position can help manage risk more effectively.

5. Leveraging Dividends and Earnings: In periods of low volatility, dividends and earnings announcements can provide temporary spikes in an otherwise flat trading landscape. By strategically positioning iron condors around these events, traders can potentially enhance premiums while still employing protective measures to guard against the increased risk associated with such events.

Risk Management Considerations

Risk management takes on heightened importance in low volatility environments. The allure of higher premiums for tighter spreads must be balanced against the increased probability of an adverse move. Employing rigorous stop-loss protocols, maintaining diversified positions across various sectors, and staying attuned to macroeconomic indicators are critical components of a comprehensive risk management strategy.

Trading iron condors in low volatility conditions requires a blend of creativity, discipline, and strategic finesse. By adjusting the structural components of the iron condor, embracing shorter expiration cycles, exercising selective judgment in underlying selection, and applying incremental adjustments, traders can navigate the serene yet deceptive waters of low volatility markets. Moreover, a steadfast commitment to meticulous risk management ensures that traders not only preserve capital but also capitalize on the nuanced opportunities presented by these quiet market phases.

Adjusting for Smaller Premiums

Strategies for dealing with smaller premiums must address the dual objectives of maximizing income potential while managing risk exposure. The following techniques are instrumental in navigating this delicate balance:

1. Enhanced Position Monitoring: With smaller premiums, the margin for error narrows, necessitating closer and more frequent monitoring of open positions. This vigilant oversight allows traders to react swiftly to market changes, enabling timely adjustments or exits before minor shifts escalate into significant threats.

2. Utilizing Credit Spreads: In strategies involving iron condors, focusing on credit spreads can be particularly advantageous when premiums are modest. By selling options with higher premiums and buying options with lower premiums, traders can collect net premiums even in a constrained market. The key lies in selecting spreads that offer the best risk-reward ratio, factoring in the probabilities of success and the potential returns relative to the risk undertaken.

3. Selective Use of Leverage: While leverage increases risk, its judicious use can amplify returns from smaller premiums. The

application of leverage must be tempered with caution, ensuring that it aligns with the trader's risk tolerance and market outlook. Employing leverage to enhance positions in high-confidence scenarios can elevate the profitability of trades that might otherwise yield minimal returns.

4. Exploiting Market Events: Events such as earnings announcements, product launches, and regulatory decisions can introduce temporary volatility into the market, potentially increasing premiums. By strategically timing iron condor trades around these events, traders can capture higher premiums. This approach demands a thorough analysis of historical data to gauge potential market reactions and a clear strategy for risk mitigation, as event-driven volatility can also lead to rapid losses.

5. Optimization through Analysis Tools: Advanced analytical tools and software can aid in identifying optimal trade setups for iron condors, especially when navigating smaller premiums. These tools can analyze vast amounts of market data, offering insights into potential premium opportunities that might be overlooked manually. Incorporating technology into the strategy enhances decision-making, enabling traders to pinpoint positions with favorable risk-reward profiles.

6. Diversification Across Time and Strategies: Diversifying not just across different underlying assets but also across various expiration periods and strategic approaches can help mitigate the impact of smaller premiums. By spreading risk across a broader spectrum, traders can stabilize returns, with successful trades compensating for those that underperform. This diversification extends to experimenting with variations of the iron condor strategy, such as adjusting strike prices or exploring asymmetrical setups, to discover configurations that

thrive under current market conditions.

While the strategies outlined offer pathways to profitability in the face of smaller premiums, traders must remain cognizant of the risks. The pursuit of higher premiums through adjustments must not lead to overexposure or deviation from sound risk management principles. Balancing the quest for returns with the imperative of capital preservation remains the cornerstone of successful trading.

Adjusting for smaller premiums within the iron condor strategy framework is an exercise in precision, innovation, and restraint. By employing enhanced monitoring, leveraging credit spreads, applying selective leverage, exploiting market events, utilizing analytical tools, and embracing diversification, traders can navigate the challenges posed by reduced premium environments. However, the overarching theme of prudent risk management must guide all strategic decisions, ensuring that the pursuit of profitability does not compromise the foundational tenets of disciplined trading.

Tighter Condors vs. Wider Condors

The spectrum between tighter and wider condors is defined by the strike price intervals of the options involved in the trade. A tighter condor has options with strike prices closer to each other, resulting in a narrower range where the trade remains profitable but also potentially higher premium receipts due to the increased risk of the position moving out of the profitable zone. Conversely, a wider condor extends the strike price intervals, offering a broader range for profitability but usually at the cost of lower premium receipts, attributed to the reduced risk of price movements leading to losses.

Tighter condors are often likened to a highwire act, requiring precision and a keen sense of market direction. The allure of tighter condors lies in their ability to generate higher premiums due to the increased risk associated with their narrower profitable range. This strategy thrives in markets characterized by low volatility, where the underlying asset's price is more likely to remain within the narrow profitable zone until expiration.

However, the precision required for executing tighter condors comes with its own set of challenges. The narrow window for profitability means there is less room for error or unexpected market movements. Thus, traders employing this strategy must exercise vigilant risk management, employing stop-loss orders and readying themselves for quick exits or adjustments if the market starts to move against their position.

On the other end of the spectrum, wider condors offer a safer passageway, granting traders a larger buffer against market volatility. The broader range between strike prices reduces the risk of the trade moving out of the profitable zone, making it an appealing strategy in markets experiencing moderate to high volatility. The sacrifice comes in the form of lower premiums compared to tighter condors, as the increased safety reduces potential returns.

Wider condors suit traders who prioritize capital preservation and risk management over maximizing returns. This approach requires patience and a long-term perspective, as returns accumulate gradually over time. Additionally, the wider spreads demand more substantial capital allocation to maintain positions, which may limit the number of trades a trader can manage simultaneously.

Choosing between tighter and wider condors involves a complex interplay of factors including market volatility, capital availability, risk tolerance, and trading objectives. Traders must also consider transaction costs, as executing four-leg strategies like iron condors incurs higher fees, which can erode profitability, especially in tighter condors where premiums are higher but profit margins thinner.

Successful iron condor trading does not adhere rigidly to one strategy over the other. Instead, it requires adaptability and the flexibility to shift between tighter and wider spreads in response to changing market conditions. This dynamic approach allows traders to optimize their position to capture the best possible premiums while managing risk effectively.

The dichotomy between tighter and wider condors represents a fundamental strategic choice in iron condor trading, each with its unique risk-reward profile. Understanding and navigating these differences is crucial for traders aiming to harness the full potential of iron condors. By carefully assessing market conditions, personal risk tolerance, and trading goals, traders can select the approach that best aligns with their strategy, whether it calls for the precision of tighter condors or the stability and sacrifice of wider ones.

The decision to sit out often hinges on the ability to read and interpret market signals accurately. Volatility indexes, such as the VIX, provide a broad measure of market sentiment and can signal periods of heightened uncertainty or complacency. A sudden spike in volatility may render the precise calculations behind an iron condor strategy null, pushing traders to the sidelines in anticipation of more stable conditions.

Economic Calendars and Earnings Announcements

Economic calendars, populated with events like central bank announcements, employment reports, and inflation data releases, are critical in planning trading activities. The weeks surrounding such events may introduce excessive volatility unsuitable for iron condor trades, which thrive in more predictable environments. Similarly, earnings announcements for companies within the index or ETF underlying the iron condor can introduce binary outcomes, making it advisable to wait until the dust settles.

For traders who incorporate technical analysis, certain chart patterns and indicators might suggest unfavorable conditions for iron condors. For instance, a breakout from a consolidation pattern could indicate a pending directional move, making it risky to establish positions predicated on the underlying asset's price remaining within a specific range. Recognizing these patterns and respecting their implications is crucial in deciding when to pause trading activities.

Psychological and Capital Considerations

Sometimes, the decision to sit out is less about market conditions and more about personal circumstances. A series of losses, for example, can impair judgment, leading to what is known as 'revenge trading'—an attempt to recuperate losses quickly, often with scant regard for strategy or risk management. In such instances, stepping back is vital for mental health and capital preservation. Additionally, if capital allocation guidelines suggest overexposure to risk, it's prudent to avoid new positions until the balance is restored.

Certain times of the year are historically more volatile than others. For instance, the end of quarters, when funds rebalance their portfolios, can see increased market movements. Similarly, historically, October has seen significant market downturns. Traders aware of these patterns might choose to reduce their exposure during these periods, opting instead to watch from the sidelines.

Flexibility and adaptability are hallmarks of successful traders. The decision to sit out should not be seen as a failure but as a strategic choice that underscores a disciplined approach to trading. Markets are in perpetual flux, and what works today may not tomorrow. Staying informed, continuously learning, and being willing to adjust strategies in response to market conditions are critical.

Choosing when to sit out is as crucial as deciding when to trade. It involves a complex interplay of market analysis, personal discipline, and strategic foresight. Iron condor traders must cultivate the ability to discern when the market's conditions align with their strategy and, perhaps more importantly, when to wait for a more opportune moment. This cautious approach not only preserves capital but also ensures that traders are ready and capable when the right conditions emerge, embodying the adage that sometimes the best action is inaction.

Event-Driven Condors: Harnessing Market Movements

The cornerstone of executing event-driven condors lies in the meticulous identification of events that are likely to induce significant market responses. These events can range from scheduled economic data releases, such as unemployment rates and consumer price index (CPI) updates, to corporate events like earnings reports, product launches, or mergers and acquisitions announcements. The key is to target events that promise a clear before-and-after impact on the volatility of the underlying asset.

Timing is paramount. The ideal window for setting up an event-driven condor is in the days leading up to the anticipated event. This period often witnesses a ramp-up in implied volatility, as market participants speculate on the outcome. By establishing positions during this build-up, traders can benefit from the heightened premiums available on options.

The positioning of strike prices requires a delicate balance. They must be set wide enough to account for the expected volatility surge, yet not so wide that the potential returns become negligible. This balancing act is informed by historical data analysis of past events of a similar nature and the prevailing market sentiment.

Post-event, the typical reaction is a sharp decline in implied volatility, a phenomenon known as volatility crush. This rapid decompression can work in favor of the iron condor trader, as the value of both the sold call and put spreads diminishes rapidly, allowing for the potential to close positions at a profit sooner than anticipated. However, the magnitude of the market's move is a critical factor; a move beyond the bounds of the condor's wings can still result in a loss, despite the volatility crush.

Event-driven condors, by their nature, introduce heightened risk given the uncertainties surrounding the event's outcome. Effective risk management strategies are crucial. These may include setting strict risk-reward parameters, utilizing stop-loss orders to exit positions that move against the trader significantly, or employing a partial close strategy to lock in profits or minimize losses as the event unfolds.

Moreover, flexibility in exit strategies is vital. While the traditional iron condor strategy may advocate for holding until expiration, the event-driven condor often necessitates a more dynamic approach, ready to capitalize on the post-event volatility crush or cut losses if the market's reaction is unexpectedly adverse.

Incorporating event-driven condors into a broader trading strategy offers a way to diversify and potentially enhance returns. However, it requires an astute understanding of market mechanisms, a keen eye for detail in event selection, and an unwavering commitment to disciplined risk management. Traders must continuously refine their approach, drawing on each experience to better navigate future events.

Event-driven condors represent a sophisticated, albeit more speculative, application of the iron condor strategy. They offer the promise of capitalizing on the volatility surrounding market events but demand a higher degree of market insight, timing precision, and risk tolerance. As with any advanced trading strategy, success with event-driven condors comes down to diligent research, meticulous planning, and the agile execution of well-conceived trades.

Earnings Announcements: The Catalysts for Strategic Iron Condor Positioning

The period leading up to earnings announcements is typically marked by a palpable increase in implied volatility, as investors and traders speculate on the company's performance. This speculative atmosphere creates an opportune environment for iron condor traders, as the elevated implied volatility inflates option premiums, making the initial setup potentially more profitable. The key lies in accurately predicting how much the stock price might swing post-announcement and positioning the condor's wings to capture this anticipated move without being overrun.

Implementing an iron condor in the context of an earnings announcement demands a nuanced strategy. Unlike traditional iron condors that thrive in low-volatility environments, earnings-driven condors must account for the expected surge in price movement. Traders often narrow the distance between strike prices, accepting a lower potential return for a higher probability of capturing the price movement within the condor's boundaries. This adjustment requires a deep dive into historical performance, analyzing how past earnings announcements have affected stock prices and implied volatility levels.

The execution phase is critical. Ideally, traders position their earnings-driven iron condors several days before the announcement, capitalizing on the pre-earnings volatility spike. The timing of entry is a delicate balance — too early, and the position may not fully benefit from rising premiums; too late, and the premiums may have already peaked.

Adjustments post-earnings are equally pivotal. The immediate aftermath of an announcement often sees a rapid contraction in implied volatility — the volatility crush. If the stock's price swing stays within the iron condor's boundaries, this volatility crush can erode the value of the sold options swiftly, allowing for an early profitable exit from the position. However, if the stock price moves aggressively beyond the condor's parameters, prompt adjustments or exits become necessary to mitigate losses.

Risk management takes on an enhanced role when trading iron condors around earnings announcements. Given the unpredictability of market reactions, setting predefined risk parameters is essential. Traders must decide in advance the maximum loss they are willing to accept and the point at which adjustments or exits will be executed. This proactive stance on risk management helps prevent emotional decision-making in the heat of market reactions.

Beyond the mechanical aspects of setting up an earnings-driven iron condor, successful traders enrich their strategy with a thorough analysis of the company in question. Understanding the business model, sector dynamics, and the broader economic context can provide additional insights into how the stock might react to its earnings announcement. This holistic approach, combining quantitative analysis with qualitative company insights, can lend an edge in the highly competitive arena of earnings-driven options trading.

Earnings announcements represent a double-edged sword in the world of options trading. While they introduce a higher level of uncertainty, they also offer the potential for heightened rewards. For the iron condor trader, earnings periods are not to be avoided but embraced, with a well-considered strategy that respects the volatility and potential price movements these events can generate. Through meticulous planning, precise execution, and disciplined risk management, traders can navigate the tumultuous waters of earnings seasons, turning potential dangers into strategic opportunities.

Federal Reserve Announcements and Economic Events: Strategic Navigations for Iron Condor Traders

Federal Reserve announcements on interest rates, monetary policy, and economic outlook can dramatically affect investor sentiment and market dynamics. These announcements can lead to a rapid recalibration of stock and options prices across the board. For the iron condor trader, the primary focus is on the anticipated volatility spike — an element that can both endanger and enhance the iron condor setup. The adept trader monitors market sentiment leading up to these announcements, seeking to understand not just the potential direction of market movement, but more crucially, the magnitude of the expected volatility.

Economic indicators such as employment reports, GDP growth figures, and inflation data also play significant roles in shaping market volatility. Similar to Federal Reserve announcements, the release of major economic data can lead to a swift and pronounced reaction within financial markets. Iron condor traders, therefore, must be adept at reading economic calendars and incorporating this information into their trading strategies. This may involve adjusting the width of the iron condor's spreads or shifting the position entirely to accommodate expected movements triggered by upcoming economic events.

The timing of entry before Federal Reserve announcements or major economic events is a delicate decision. Traders might opt to set up an iron condor well before the event to capitalize on the rising implied volatility, thus securing higher premiums. However, this approach comes with the risk of significant market swings post-announcement, which could breach the condor's boundaries. Alternatively, entering a position after the event allows traders to assess the market's direction and volatility more clearly but may result in lower premiums due to the volatility crush.

Risk management strategies must be meticulously planned and rigorously adhered to, especially in these high-stakes scenarios. This includes setting stop-loss orders, being prepared for quick adjustments, or even choosing to close positions early to preserve capital. Successful traders often run scenario analyses, preparing for multiple outcomes based on the announcement's content and the market's subsequent reactions.

The aftermath of Federal Reserve announcements and economic events presents unique opportunities for iron condor traders. The initial volatility surge often subsides within a few days, a phenomenon known as the "volatility crush." Skilled traders can take advantage of this by setting positions that benefit from the rapid decline in option premiums, provided the market's reaction stays within the bounds of the iron condor's strike prices.

A comprehensive understanding of the broader economic landscape is invaluable in these situations. Traders who keep abreast of not just individual announcements but also the general economic climate can better anticipate market movements. This includes understanding the current stage of the economic cycle, investor sentiment, and the interplay between different sectors of the economy. Such insights can guide the strategic adjustments to iron condor positions in the face of macroeconomic events.

Geopolitical Events and Their Impacts: Maneuvering Through Global Uncertainty

Geopolitical events encompass a broad spectrum of occurrences, from escalating military conflicts and political upheavals to significant policy changes and international trade agreements.

Each event carries the potential to sway investor sentiment and trigger fluctuations in market prices, impacting sectors unevenly and creating a ripple effect across global markets. For iron condor traders, the challenge lies in predicting not only the direction of market movement in response to these events but also the scale and duration of their impact.

The approach to managing iron condor positions in the face of geopolitical uncertainty hinges on a deep understanding of risk exposure and a robust strategy for adjustment and containment. Traders might consider tightening their spreads to reduce potential losses or shifting their positions to more stable sectors less affected by geopolitical strife. Proactive monitoring of news and analyst forecasts becomes crucial, as timely information can be the difference between a strategic retreat and a costly oversight.

Effective risk management under the shadow of geopolitical events requires a multifaceted approach. Hedging strategies, such as employing protective puts or diversifying across non-correlated assets, can provide a safety net against unforeseen market gyrations. Additionally, setting precise stop-loss orders and having a clear exit strategy for positions can help mitigate losses when markets react sharply to geopolitical news.

Amidst the challenges posed by geopolitical events, there lie opportunities for the keen-eyed trader. The initial market overreactions often lead to mispricings and anomalies in option premiums, presenting lucrative opportunities for iron condor traders to enter positions at favorable prices. Furthermore, post-event market stabilization often brings a "volatility crush," enabling traders to benefit from the decline in option premiums if their positions are strategically placed and well-managed.

A nuanced understanding of the geopolitical landscape is indispensable for traders seeking to navigate these events profitably. This includes being aware of the historical context, the interests of different stakeholders, and the potential for escalation or resolution. Traders who can anticipate the market's sentiment towards various outcomes can better position their iron condors to withstand volatility or capitalize on resultant trends.

Geopolitical events present a complex array of challenges and opportunities for iron condor traders. By employing a strategic blend of meticulous planning, proactive risk management, and informed speculation, traders can navigate the uncertainties of global events. This involves not only guarding against potential market downturns but also recognizing and seizing opportunities that such volatility may unveil. In the dance of options trading against the backdrop of global events, the most successful traders are those who remain vigilant, adaptable, and always informed.

Position Management and Adjustment Techniques: Navigating with Precision and Strategy

Position management begins with a clear understanding of one's initial setup parameters, including the desired risk-reward ratio, the width of the spreads, and the selection of strike prices relative to current market conditions. The key to effective management lies in the trader's ability to monitor these positions against a backdrop of market volatility and time decay, making adjustments that align with their evolving risk tolerance and market outlook.

Adjustment Techniques for Iron Condors

Adjustments in iron condor positions are typically necessitated by significant market movements that threaten the potential profitability or risk thresholds set by the trader. Several techniques stand out for their utility:

1. Rolling Out: This involves moving a position to a further expiration date, granting the market more time to revert to a favorable status. This technique is particularly useful when a trader believes in the eventual profitability of their position but seeks to avoid short-term volatility.

2. Rolling Up/Down: Applied to either the put or call side of the condor, this adjustment involves closing a part of the position that is under threat and opening a new position at a different strike price. This maneuver seeks to reduce potential losses or lock in profits while maintaining exposure to the market.

3. Unwinding Part of the Spread: In scenarios where one side of the iron condor is significantly outperforming the other, a trader might choose to close the profitable leg, thereby reducing the overall risk and locking in partial profits.

4. Doubling Down: This high-risk strategy involves adding a new iron condor setup when the existing position moves against the trader. It's predicated on the belief that the market will reverse its course, allowing both positions to become profitable. However, this approach requires careful risk assessment, as it doubles the potential exposure.

Integrating Delta and Gamma for Precision Adjustments

The Greeks, particularly Delta and Gamma, serve as critical

indicators for adjusting iron condor positions. Delta, which measures the rate of change of an option's price relative to a $1 change in the underlying asset, guides traders in understanding how close their positions are to being challenged. Gamma, the rate of change in Delta, helps anticipate how quickly adjustments may be needed as market conditions evolve.

A delta-neutral strategy aims to adjust positions such that the overall delta of the iron condor is brought close to zero, minimizing sensitivity to small price movements. Meanwhile, managing gamma involves making adjustments to control how delta changes, ensuring that the position remains relatively stable even as the market fluctuates.

Implementing Stop Losses and Alerts

The use of stop losses and setting up alerts based on technical indicators or market news can be instrumental in position management. These tools allow traders to set predefined conditions under which their positions will be automatically adjusted or closed, reducing the emotional strain and maintaining discipline in the face of market unpredictability.

CHAPTER 5: POSITION MANAGEMENT AND ADJUSTMENT TECHNIQUES

Delta represents the rate of change in an option's price relative to a $1 change in the underlying asset's price. It's the first derivative of the option pricing model concerning the underlying asset's price. In the context of iron condors, understanding Delta is paramount, as it provides insight into how exposed an iron condor position is to movements in the underlying market. A positive Delta indicates a position benefits from an uptick in the market, while a negative Delta suggests an advantage when the market declines.

For iron condor traders, maintaining a Delta-neutral position is often the Grail quest - a state where the portfolio is theoretically immune to small movements in the underlying asset's price. Achieving this requires adept adjustments, guided by the Delta's whispers. For instance, should a sudden market movement skew the Delta away from neutrality, a trader might adjust their position by adding or removing options to rebalance the Delta, thereby restoring equilibrium and minimizing directional risk.

Gamma: The Custodian of Convexity

While Delta tracks price sensitivity, Gamma is the second derivative of the option pricing model, measuring the rate of change of Delta itself. It's a gauge of the stability of an option's Delta, and by extension, the predictability of an option's price movement. In the iron condor setup, where multiple options across different strike prices are juggled, Gamma's role becomes critically important.

A high Gamma in an iron condor position suggests that Delta is highly sensitive to changes in the underlying asset's price. This can be both a boon and a bane. On one side, a favorable market move can significantly amplify profits as the Delta's change magnifies the position's sensitivity to the market's direction. Conversely, an adverse move can just as rapidly erode the position's value, making high Gamma positions a high-stakes game, necessitating vigilant adjustments to manage risk.

Strategic Adjustments with Delta and Gamma

Adjusting an iron condor position in light of Delta and Gamma involves a delicate balancing act. Traders might employ various techniques, such as 'Delta hedging', where additional positions are taken to offset Delta's movement, thus reducing the portfolio's sensitivity to the underlying price changes. Conversely, managing Gamma might involve restructuring the iron condor to positions with lower Gamma, reducing the impact of rapid Delta changes on the portfolio.

Moreover, adjustments are not solely reactive but can also

be proactive. Anticipating events that might spike volatility, traders can preemptively adjust their Delta and Gamma exposures, positioning themselves to either capitalize on the expected market movements or insulate their portfolio against potential downturns.

Understanding and adjusting for Delta and Gamma within iron condor strategies are akin to mastering the winds and currents in the vast ocean of options trading. These metrics not only inform the trader of the present state of their positions but also guide the necessary adjustments to navigate through market volatility. Mastering these adjustments, informed by the dynamic interplay of Delta and Gamma, is essential for any trader aspiring to craft robust, resilient iron condor strategies that can withstand the market's capricious nature. Through meticulous attention to these Greeks, traders can transform unpredictable market movements into strategic opportunities, steering their iron condors toward profitable horizons.

Delta Neutral Strategies

Delta neutrality is a methodological stance wherein the total Delta of a portfolio is meticulously balanced to zero, or as close to it as possible. The primary objective is to construct a position that is ostensibly indifferent to small fluctuations in the underlying asset's price. This is achieved by balancing positive and negative Delta positions, ensuring that the portfolio's overall sensitivity to price movements is neutralized. In the dynamic landscape of iron condor trading, Delta neutrality is pursued to mitigate exposure to directional risk, allowing the trader to focus on profiting from volatility and time decay.

The inception of a Delta neutral iron condor begins with the selection of call and put options that, when combined, offset each other's Delta. The iron condor, a strategy that involves selling out-of-the-money call and put spreads, inherently possesses a degree of Delta neutrality due to its symmetrical construction. However, achieving perfect Delta neutrality requires fine-tuning—adjustments that might include altering the strike prices or quantities of the options involved in the spreads.

The quest for Delta neutrality is not a one-time endeavor but a continuous journey. As the market ebbs and flows, the Delta of individual options within the iron condor will invariably shift, nudging the overall position away from neutrality. The adept trader responds with surgical precision, executing adjustments to reestablish equilibrium. These adjustments might involve rolling out-of-the-money options closer to the money, thus increasing their Delta, or adding new positions to counteract the imbalance.

While Delta provides the direction, Gamma measures the path's curvature. In Delta neutral strategies, Gamma signifies the rate at which Delta changes as the underlying price moves. High Gamma indicates that Delta neutrality can be fleeting, requiring frequent adjustments to maintain. Therefore, managing Gamma becomes paramount in sustaining Delta neutrality over time. Traders may opt for options with lower Gamma to reduce the frequency of adjustments or may employ Gamma hedging strategies to further stabilize their position.

The ultimate aim of Delta neutral strategies in iron condor trading is not merely to exist unscathed by market movements but to thrive within them. By achieving Delta neutrality, traders aim to capitalize on the other facets of options trading—namely, theta decay and implied volatility. As time progresses, the value of the options decays, benefiting the sold positions in the iron condor structure. Simultaneously, changes in implied volatility can be exploited, as Delta neutral positions can be adjusted to take advantage of discrepancies between realized and implied volatility.

Delta neutral strategies embody the meticulous balance between action and inaction, a zen-like state in the volatile world of options trading. For the iron condor trader, mastering the art of Delta neutrality offers a path to mitigating directional risk, allowing the focus to shift towards the exploitation of time decay and volatility. Through continuous adjustment and a keen understanding of the interplay between Delta and Gamma, the Delta neutral iron condor becomes not just a strategy, but a dynamic narrative of adaptation and equilibrium in the pursuit of profitability.

Managing Gamma Risk

Gamma, in its essence, is the rate of change in an option's Delta for a one-point move in the underlying asset's price. It's the acceleration, the force that propels Delta, and consequently, it's a measure of the stability—or volatility—of that Delta. For iron condor traders, where the strategy hinges on the balance and neutrality of Delta, Gamma becomes a potent indicator of risk. High Gamma values suggest that the option's Delta, and thus the portfolio's directional exposure, can change rapidly with even slight fluctuations in the underlying market price. Gamma represents the fragility of balance, the potential for sudden shifts that can unsettle a meticulously constructed iron condor position.

Strategies for Managing Gamma Risk

The challenge and art of managing Gamma risk lie in the preemptive adjustments and strategic foresight. Here are key strategies employed by seasoned traders:

1. Option Selection: Preferring options with lower Gamma values for the core of the iron condor can provide a buffer against rapid Delta shifts. These options, typically those with longer expiration times or those that are further out-of-the-money, exhibit less sensitivity to price changes in the short term.

2. Dynamic Adjustments: Proactive portfolio management is essential in Gamma risk management. Traders should remain vigilant, ready to make adjustments to their positions in response to significant changes in Gamma. This may involve rebalancing the iron condor's legs—adjusting strike prices or quantities—or adding counterpositions to dampen Gamma's impact.

3. Gamma Hedging: In some instances, incorporating Gamma hedges can cushion the portfolio against undesirable Gamma fluctuations. This could involve taking positions in options with opposing Gamma exposures or utilizing dynamic hedging strategies that adjust to market movements, aiming to neutralize Gamma's effect.

Gamma and Volatility: A Dual Dance

An underlying factor influencing Gamma is implied volatility. Options with high implied volatility typically exhibit higher Gamma, as the expected wide swings in the underlying price amplify the potential for rapid changes in Delta. Thus, a comprehensive Gamma management strategy also entails navigating the terrain of volatility—anticipating periods of high volatility and adjusting the iron condor strategy accordingly. In periods of expected high volatility, traders might opt for a wider iron condor spread to accommodate larger price movements without necessitating constant adjustments.

Gamma's impact is not static; it ebbs and flows with the passage of time toward option expiration. As expiration approaches, Gamma of at-the-money options escalates, making the option's Delta more sensitive to price changes. This phenomenon, known as Gamma decay, necessitates a more hands-on approach in the final stages of the iron condor's lifecycle. Traders may need to intensify their monitoring and adjustment efforts during this period to maintain the desired risk profile.

The management of Gamma risk is a delicate art that requires a blend of analytical foresight, strategic adjustment, and an intimate understanding of the interplay between Gamma and other market forces. For the iron condor trader, mastering Gamma risk is paramount to sustaining profitability, as it directly influences the stability and predictability of the strategy's performance. Through diligent management and strategic acumen, traders can navigate the vagaries of Gamma, turning a potential source of volatility into a cornerstone of stability in their options trading odyssey.

Real-Life Examples of Adjustments

Case Study 1: The Sudden Market Drop

Imagine a scenario where a trader, Alex, has established an iron condor position on XYZ stock, which has been trading within a stable range. However, unforeseen geopolitical tensions escalate over a weekend, resulting in a significant gap down in the stock price as the market opens on Monday.

Initial Position:

- Sell 10 contracts of XYZ 100/105 call spread and 10 contracts of XYZ 95/90 put spread.

Market Reaction:

- XYZ stock drops 10% at market open.

Adjustment Strategy:

Faced with a challenged put spread now dangerously close to being in-the-money, Alex decides to roll down the call spread to collect additional premium and reduce the delta exposure on the put side.

- Adjustment: Buy back the 100/105 call spread and sell a 90/95 call spread.

This adjustment does not only collect additional premium but also balances the deltas, reducing the directional risk on the position. The extra premium collected partially offsets the loss on the put spread, demonstrating the importance of flexibility and prompt action in response to market movements.

Case Study 2: The Unexpected Rally

In another instance, let's consider Jamie, who has an iron condor position on ABC stock ahead of a scheduled earnings announcement. Contrary to expectations, the company announces breakthrough earnings, and the stock surges in after-hours trading.

Initial Position:

- Sell 10 contracts of ABC 200/205 call spread and 10 contracts of ABC 195/190 put spread.

Market Reaction:

- ABC stock surges 15% following the earnings announcement.

Adjustment Strategy:

With the call spread now deep in-the-money and facing significant losses, Jamie opts to close the put spread for a nominal gain and roll up the call spread to higher strikes while extending the expiration date.

- Adjustment: Close the 195/190 put spread and roll the 200/205 call spread to a 215/220 call spread with a later expiration.

This maneuver allows Jamie to capture more premium, potentially offsetting the loss on the call spread while giving the position more time for the stock to possibly retract within the new range. It exemplifies how extending the duration and adjusting the strikes of the affected side of an iron condor can recoup losses in the face of adverse movements.

These real-life scenarios underscore the pragmatism needed in the iron condor strategy. The ability to make judicious adjustments in response to unanticipated market events is pivotal. It involves a deep understanding of the Greeks, particularly Delta and Gamma, and how they interplay with market volatility. The examples provided demonstrate that while iron condors are designed to be neutral strategies, they require active management and an astute sense of when and how to adjust. This hands-on approach to adjustments not only mitigates risks but also enhances the chances of maintaining profitability across varying market conditions.

The Use of Beta Weighting for Portfolio Balancing

In the landscape of options trading, particularly within the domain of iron condors, an advanced technique known as beta weighting becomes instrumental for portfolio balancing. This sophisticated strategy ensures traders can maintain a holistic view of their risk exposure across various positions, irrespective of the underlying assets' nature or volatility. Diving into beta weighting requires a blend of theoretical understanding and practical application, a balance that we shall explore through the lens of iron condor adjustments.

Beta weighting is a method used by traders to assess the overall directional risk of a portfolio of stocks or options in relation to a specific benchmark, usually a well-known market index like the S&P 500. It converts the beta values of individual securities— which measure the volatility of a security in comparison to the market—into a unified risk metric. This conversion facilitates a comparative analysis against the market as a whole, enabling traders to understand how their portfolio would theoretically perform in various market conditions.

For iron condor traders, beta weighting serves as a compass navigating through the stormy seas of market volatility. It allows the trader to quantify the aggregate exposure of their positions to market movements and to make informed adjustments to maintain a desired level of neutrality or directional bias.

Real-life Scenario: Balancing with Beta Weighting

Consider Jordan, a seasoned trader managing a diversified portfolio including multiple iron condor positions across different sectors and underlying assets. The challenge arises when there's a sudden bullish trend in the market, primarily affecting the tech sector, leading to increased exposure on the call side of Jordan's iron condors.

Initial Assessment:

- Jordan's portfolio is composed of iron condors on tech, energy, and consumer goods stocks.

- The recent market rally, especially in tech stocks, skews the delta of the portfolio positively, indicating an unwanted bullish exposure.

Beta Weighting Strategy:

- Jordan calculates the beta-weighted delta of the entire portfolio against the S&P 500 index to gauge the overall market exposure.

- Discovering a higher-than-comfortable positive delta, Jordan decides to adjust.

Portfolio Adjustment:

- Reduction of Bullish Bias: Jordan opts to close out some of the call spreads in the tech sector iron condors that have moved significantly in-the-money.

- Rebalancing with New Positions: To counterbalance the reduced exposure, Jordan also initiates new iron condor positions in sectors showing less correlation with the ongoing bullish trend, after carefully beta weighting them against the S&P 500.

Outcome:

- The adjustments bring the portfolio's beta-weighted delta closer to zero, realigning with Jordan's original strategy of maintaining a market-neutral stance.

- This recalibration ensures that the portfolio's performance becomes less sensitive to specific sector movements, adhering to the diversified, balanced approach inherent in successful iron condor trading.

Beta weighting is not just a theoretical construct but a pivotal tool in the arsenal of iron condor traders. It bridges the gap between individual position management and overall portfolio performance, ensuring that a trader's exposure aligns with their strategic objectives. By meticulously applying beta weighting, traders can adeptly maneuver through market vicissitudes, maintaining the equilibrium of their portfolios and safeguarding against disproportionate risk exposure. Through practical application and continuous learning, the mastery of beta weighting becomes a cornerstone in achieving long-term success and stability in the volatile world of options trading.

Understanding Beta Weighting

Beta weighting transforms the myriad of individual position risks in a portfolio into a cohesive, comprehensible gauge against a market index, typically the S&P 500. The essence of beta weighting pivots on its ability to translate different securities' volatilities and correlations into a single metric, offering a macroscopic view of how a portfolio is positioned relative to market movements.

Iron condor traders, navigating through the labyrinth of market volatilities, utilize beta weighting to maintain a strategic equilibrium. The inherent design of iron condors aims for a market-neutral stance, yet individual legs of these options strategies can exhibit disparate sensitivities to market shifts. Herein lies the value of beta weighting, enabling traders to aggregate these sensitivities into a comprehensive risk profile.

Let's consider Evelyn, an adept trader with a penchant for iron condors, who finds herself amid fluctuating market conditions. Her portfolio spans across various sectors, each with unique beta values signifying their market volatility relation. Evelyn's goal: to sustain a balanced portfolio that mirrors the stability of an iron condor's flight amidst financial gusts.

Initial Analysis:

- Evelyn assesses her portfolio, noting the disproportionate impact of a bearish trend on her consumer sector positions.

- Each position's beta, reflecting its volatility against market swings, presents a scattered risk landscape.

Employing Beta Weighting:

- By calculating a beta-weighted delta for her portfolio, Evelyn translates individual risks into a singular metric against the S&P 500, revealing an unintended bearish tilt.

- This panoramic risk vista, illuminated by beta weighting, guides her to the crux of imbalance.

Strategic Rebalancing:

- Mitigating Bearish Overtones: Evelyn strategically unwinds some put spreads in the overly affected consumer sector positions, thereby reducing excessive negative delta.

- Harmonizing Portfolio Exposure: She augments her portfolio with additional iron condor positions in sectors demonstrating resilience or inverse correlation to current trends, after a meticulous beta-weighted analysis.

Achieving Equilibrium:

- These recalibrations, enlightened by beta weighting, steer Evelyn's portfolio towards a rebalanced state, aligning with her strategic vision of market neutrality.

- Such adept application of beta weighting not only tempers the portfolio's market sensitivity but also fortifies its strategy alignment, encapsulating the essence of prudent iron condor trading.

Understanding and applying beta weighting transcends mere risk assessment; it embodies a strategic foresight in portfolio management. For iron condor traders, mastering this concept is not an option but a necessity, facilitating a harmonious balance between individual position nuances and overarching market dynamics. Through the lens of beta weighting, traders like Evelyn decode the complex narrative of market risks into a coherent strategy, ensuring their portfolios not only endure but thrive in the multifaceted world of options trading.

Applying Beta Weighting to Iron Condor Positions

Beta weighting, a linchpin in portfolio management, becomes particularly potent when applied to the nuanced strategy of iron condors. Given the iron condor's reliance on market stability, understanding and adjusting for market exposure becomes paramount. Through beta weighting, traders can achieve a panoramic understanding of how aggregated positions might react to broader market movements, allowing for preemptive adjustments that align with their risk appetite and strategic objectives.

Imagine Jordan, a seasoned trader, who meticulously curates a portfolio of iron condors across various sectors. Jordan's objective is clear: to maintain a market-neutral stance, ensuring that his portfolio remains unaffected by minor market fluctuations.

Initial Positioning:

- Jordan's portfolio, diverse in its holdings, initially shows a skewed exposure towards tech, a sector known for its high beta, or market sensitivity.

- Without intervention, a tech rally or crash could disproportionately affect his portfolio's performance, undermining the market neutrality essential to the iron condor strategy.

Application of Beta Weighting:

- By applying beta weighting, Jordan assesses his portfolio's collective delta in relation to the broader market, embodied by the S&P 500 index.

- This assessment reveals an inadvertent bullish bias, with the tech sector's high beta amplifying the portfolio's market sensitivity.

Strategic Portfolio Adjustment:

- Sector Diversification: Jordan decides to diversify, introducing iron condors in lower-beta sectors such as utilities and consumer staples, inherently more stable and less responsive to market gyrations.

- Position Sizing: He adjusts the size of his tech sector iron condors, reducing exposure to high-beta stocks, thereby decreasing the overall market sensitivity of his portfolio.

Fine-Tuning for Market Neutrality:

- Beta-Weighted Reevaluation: Post-adjustment, Jordan revisits his portfolio's beta-weighted delta, ensuring the modifications have effectively neutralized the market exposure.

- Continuous Monitoring: Recognizing the dynamic nature of market sensitivity, Jordan commits to regular reviews of his portfolio's beta weighting, ready to make further adjustments as market conditions evolve.

Enhanced Portfolio Resilience:

Through judicious application of beta weighting, Jordan's portfolio attains a closer approximation of market neutrality. This strategic alignment not only mitigates the impact of market volatility on his iron condor positions but also optimizes the structural advantage of the strategy, focusing on generating returns through theta decay rather than directional bets.

The application of beta weighting to iron condor positions transcends basic risk management, embodying a dynamic strategy for achieving and maintaining market neutrality. For traders embarking on the iron condor strategy, mastery of beta weighting is indispensable, serving as both shield and compass in navigating the vicissitudes of financial markets. Through careful analysis and strategic portfolio adjustments, traders can harness the full potential of iron condors, crafting a portfolio that is not only resilient but poised for success in the multifaceted arena of options trading.

How to Achieve a Balanced Portfolio

A balanced portfolio, in the context of options trading, is one that optimally mitigates risk while aiming for consistent returns. It necessitates a harmonious blend of strategies, asset classes, and market exposures. The iron condor, with its inherent design for neutral market conditions, plays a pivotal role in such a portfolio, serving as a stabilizer amidst the ebbs and flows of market volatility.

Diversification, the cornerstone of portfolio balance, extends beyond mere asset allocation. It encompasses strategic diversity. For instance, while iron condors excel in low volatility, incorporating strategies that thrive in high volatility environments, such as straddles or strangles, ensures the portfolio is equipped to navigate varying market conditions.

Example: Emily's Portfolio Adjustment:

Consider Emily, an astute trader, who seeks to refine her portfolio's balance. Initially heavily weighted towards iron condors, her portfolio performs admirably in stable markets but suffers during unexpected volatility spikes.

- Strategic Expansion: Emily introduces dynamic straddle positions, capitalizing on her forecast of a volatile earnings season. This strategic diversification allows her to harness market movements, irrespective of direction.

- Risk Assessment: Meticulously, she assesses the risk profile of each position, leveraging tools like delta and gamma measurements to understand her portfolio's exposure to price movements and volatility.

- Correlation Analysis: Emily evaluates the correlation between her holdings, aiming for a collection of strategies and assets that do not move in lockstep. Through this, she enhances the resilience of her portfolio against market downturns.

Leveraging Technology for Balance:

In today's digital age, traders have at their disposal sophisticated tools for portfolio analysis and balance assessment. Software platforms can automatically analyze the risk parameters of a portfolio, offering insights into potential adjustments for better balance.

- Technology in Practice: Utilizing a trading platform, Emily simulates various market scenarios to gauge the potential impact on her portfolio. This predictive analysis informs her decision-making process, guiding her towards adjustments that enhance balance and mitigate risk.

The Role of Continuous Learning and Adaptation:

Achieving a balanced portfolio is not a one-time endeavor but a continuous process of learning and adaptation. The markets are ever-changing, and strategies that were once profitable may no longer align with current conditions.

- Market Research: Keeping abreast of market trends and economic indicators allows traders to preemptively adjust their portfolios in anticipation of shifts in volatility or market sentiment.

- Education: Engaging with the trading community, attending workshops, and consuming financial literature are invaluable for gaining fresh perspectives and insights into portfolio balancing techniques.

Achieving a balanced portfolio in options trading is a dynamic and nuanced process. It demands a strategic blend of diversification, risk management, and continuous adaptation. By incorporating varied strategies like iron condors and leveraging technological tools for analysis, traders can construct portfolios that not only withstand the test of market fluctuations but also thrive within them. This journey towards balance, underscored by education and strategic foresight, empowers traders to navigate the complexities of financial markets with confidence and acumen.

Hedging Your Bets: Protective Strategies

Hedging, involves taking an offsetting or opposite position in a related security to mitigate the risk of adverse price movements in the original investment. In the context of options trading, and particularly within strategies like the iron condor, hedging becomes a nuanced art that requires both foresight and precision.

One fundamental approach to hedging is diversification—not just in the assets one holds but also in the hedging instruments themselves. For an iron condor trader, this might mean employing protective puts or calls on the underlying asset, diversifying with positions in correlated or inversely correlated assets, or utilizing index options for broad market protection.

Case Study: Alex's Approach to Hedging:

Alex, a prudent trader with a penchant for iron condors, recognizes the importance of hedging in his trading regimen. He meticulously employs a combination of protective puts and index options to hedge his portfolio.

- Protective Puts: Alex buys puts on the same underlying asset of his iron condors. These puts increase in value if the asset's price falls, offsetting losses from his iron condor positions.

- Index Options: Given that Alex's portfolio is heavily skewed towards tech stocks, he hedges against sector-wide downturns by purchasing puts on a major tech index. This strategy provides broad market protection, cushioning his portfolio against systemic risks.

Technological Leverage in Hedging:

In an era where technology permeates every facet of trading, traders employ sophisticated software to aid in hedging strategies. These tools can analyze portfolio risk in real-time, suggest appropriate hedges, and even automate hedging actions based on predetermined criteria.

- Real-Time Analytics: By utilizing platforms that offer real-time portfolio analytics, Alex can dynamically adjust his hedging strategies in response to market movements, ensuring optimal protection.

- Automated Hedging: To streamline his hedging process, Alex sets up automated triggers on his trading platform. These triggers automatically initiate hedging positions when certain risk thresholds are breached, ensuring that his portfolio is protected even when he's not actively monitoring the markets.

Hedging is not a 'set it and forget it' strategy. It requires ongoing adjustment and adaptation to evolving market conditions. As such, successful traders like Alex continuously reassess their hedging positions, taking into account new market data, changes in the economic landscape, and shifts in their own investment objectives.

Protective strategies, with hedging being paramount among them, are indispensable in the toolkit of the modern options trader. They provide a safeguard against the inherent risks of the market, allowing traders to pursue their strategic objectives with a greater sense of security. Through a combination of diversification, technological leverage, and continuous adaptation, traders can construct a robust hedging framework that supports their broader trading strategies while protecting against downside risk. As we navigate the complex and often turbulent waters of the financial markets, these protective strategies light the way, offering a beacon of stability and reassurance.

Using Index Options for Broad Market Protection

Index options are derivatives based on the value of market indices, such as the S&P 500 or the NASDAQ-100. Unlike options on individual stocks, index options provide exposure to the entire market or specific sectors, thus offering a protective shield against systemic risks that can affect multiple securities simultaneously.

Utilizing index options for hedging involves a strategic approach tailored to the portfolio's exposure and the trader's risk tolerance. For instance, if a significant portion of a trader's portfolio is composed of technology stocks, purchasing put options on the NASDAQ-100 index could serve as an effective hedge against sector-wide downturns.

Case Study: Brenda's Hedging Strategy with Index Options:

Brenda, an experienced trader with a diverse portfolio, recognises the vulnerability of her investments to broader market corrections. To mitigate this, she adopts a dual-strategy:

- S&P 500 Put Options: Aware of her portfolio's alignment with the overall market, Brenda purchases put options on the S&P 500 index. This strategy provides a safety net, ensuring that any broad market downturns are partially offset by gains from the put options.

- Sector-Specific Hedges: For her tech-heavy investments, Brenda also buys put options on the NASDAQ-100. This serves as a targeted hedge, protecting against declines specific to the technology sector.

Integration with Iron Condor Positions:

For traders employing iron condor strategies, index options add an extra layer of defence. Iron condors, by design, thrive in a market with low volatility. However, sudden market-wide events can disrupt this balance. By incorporating index options as part of the hedging strategy, traders can shield their positions from unexpected volatility spikes.

- Dynamic Hedging: Brenda periodically reviews her index option positions, adjusting them based on changes in her portfolio and shifts in market sentiment. This dynamic hedging approach allows her to maintain an optimal balance between risk and reward.

Technological Support for Strategy Implementation:

Advancements in trading platforms have streamlined the process of implementing complex strategies like index option hedging. These platforms offer features such as:

- Risk Analysis Tools: Traders can use these tools to assess the impact of market movements on their portfolio and identify the optimal index options for hedging.

- Automated Alerts and Execution: By setting up automated alerts for specific market conditions, traders can execute hedging strategies promptly, ensuring they are always one step ahead of market movements.

Using index options for broad market protection is a sophisticated strategy that complements the nuanced approaches of options trading, particularly within iron condors. It empowers traders to navigate the uncertainties of financial markets with confidence, knowing that their portfolios have an added layer of security against systemic risks. Whether faced with sector-wide downturns or market-wide corrections, the strategic use of index options stands as a testament to the power of informed, proactive risk management. Through careful planning, ongoing adjustment, and leveraging cutting-edge technology, traders can harness the protective potential of index options, safeguarding their investments against the unpredictable tides of the market.

Individual Stock Hedging Techniques

The rationale behind individual stock hedging is straightforward: to safeguard the value of investments in scenarios where a particular stock might experience a downturn. This necessity becomes especially poignant for traders with significant exposure to a single stock or sector, where the idiosyncratic risks—those unique to a specific company or industry—can pose a substantial threat to their portfolio's overall health.

Techniques for Hedging Individual Stocks:

1. Protective Puts: This classic hedging strategy involves buying put options on a stock that one owns. the put option acts as an insurance policy, setting a floor on the potential losses from the owned stock. If the stock's price plummets below the strike price of the put option, the trader can exercise the option, selling the stock at the strike price, thus mitigating the loss.

2. Covered Calls: While primarily used as an income-generating strategy, writing covered calls can also serve as a hedge. By selling call options on stock that they own, traders receive a premium, which provides a cushion against a potential decline in the stock's price. However, this strategy caps the upside potential, which is a trade-off that traders must consider.

3. Collars: A collar strategy combines protective puts and covered calls to hedge a stock position. A trader buys a protective put while simultaneously writing a covered call on the same

stock, with both options typically having the same expiration date. This approach not only provides downside protection but also helps finance the cost of the put option with the premium received from the call option.

Case Study: Alex's Hedging Strategy on XYZ Corp:

Alex holds a significant position in XYZ Corp, a tech company known for its volatility. Concerned about an upcoming earnings report that could send the stock tumbling, Alex decides to implement a collar strategy:

- Protective Put: Alex buys puts with a strike price 5% below XYZ's current market price, securing a minimum sell price should the stock plunge.

- Covered Call: Simultaneously, Alex writes call options with a strike price 5% above the current market price, willing to cap gains for added protection and income from the call premium.

- Outcome: The earnings report reveals unexpected challenges, causing XYZ's stock to drop. However, the protective put minimizes Alex's losses, while the premium from the covered call offsets part of the cost of buying the put.

Adapting Strategies to Market Conditions:

Individual stock hedging is not a set-it-and-forget-it strategy. Traders must continually assess the market conditions, earnings reports, and sector news to adjust their hedging techniques accordingly. For instance, in a bullish market, traders might lean towards covered calls for additional income, whereas, in a bearish or volatile market, protective puts become more appealing for their downside protection.

Individual stock hedging is an essential tool in the options trader's arsenal, offering a bespoke shield against the ebbs and flows of stock-specific risks. By judiciously applying techniques such as protective puts, covered calls, and collars, traders can navigate the uncertain waters of the stock market with greater confidence and control. Moreover, integrating these strategies within a broader trading plan, including iron condor positions and index option hedges, creates a multi-faceted defense, maximizing protection while striving for substantial returns.

When and How to Apply Different Hedges

The decision to apply a particular hedging strategy hinges on several factors, including market sentiment, individual stock performance, and the broader economic landscape. A nuanced understanding of these elements enables traders to tailor their hedging approaches to current conditions, maximizing their effectiveness.

1. Market Sentiment and Volatility: In times of high volatility or bearish market sentiment, traders often lean towards protective puts due to their direct downside protection. Conversely, in a bullish or stable market, covered calls may be preferred for generating income while offering a degree of hedging.

2. Individual Stock Performance: The performance and volatility of the specific stock in question are critical. For stocks with high volatility, a collar strategy might be the best approach, providing a balanced mechanism for protection and potential income.

3. Economic Landscape: Broader economic indicators, such as interest rates, inflation data, and geopolitical events, can influence market conditions. Traders must adapt their hedging strategies to anticipate or react to these macroeconomic factors.

When to Apply Different Hedges:

- Before Earnings Announcements: Volatility typically spikes around earnings announcements. Traders holding positions in stocks about to report earnings might favor protective puts or collars to hedge against unexpected moves.

- During Bullish Trends: In a sustained bull market, writing covered calls against owned stocks can generate income while still participating in the market's upside, albeit with a cap on potential gains.

- In Bearish Phases: In a downturn, protective puts become invaluable, offering a safety net against declining stock prices. This strategy is particularly pertinent for traders looking to preserve capital in a depreciating market.

How to Apply Different Hedges:

- Timing: The timing of hedge implementation is crucial. Ideally, hedges should be set up when the cost of doing so (e.g., the premium for options) is relatively low, which often means acting before volatility spikes.

- Selection of Strike Prices and Expiration Dates: The choice of strike prices and expiration dates for options used in hedging strategies should align with the trader's risk tolerance and market outlook. For protective puts, a strike price at or slightly below the current stock price offers more protection but at a higher cost. Similarly, the expiration date should provide enough time to cover the anticipated period of risk.

- Adjustments: Hedging isn't a one-time setup; it requires ongoing adjustments. For example, if a stock's price moves significantly, a trader might need to roll up the strike price of covered calls or adjust the protective puts to ensure adequate coverage.

Case Study: Emma's Hedging Decision During Market Turbulence:

Emma, an experienced trader, holds a diversified portfolio but is particularly concerned about her substantial position in ABC Tech ahead of a volatile election period. Expecting increased market turbulence, she decides to implement a collar strategy on ABC Tech. By selecting put options with a strike price 10% below the current level and selling call options with a strike price 10% above, Emma creates a hedging structure that protects against significant downside while allowing for some upside potential. As the market indeed turns volatile, ABC Tech's stock fluctuates wildly, but Emma's position remains relatively insulated from extreme movements, showcasing the effectiveness of timely and well-considered hedging.

The application of hedging techniques in options trading is both an art and a science, requiring a deep understanding of market dynamics, a keen sense of timing, and the ability to adapt to changing conditions. By judiciously choosing when and how to employ strategies such as protective puts, covered calls, and collars, traders can shield their investments from unexpected downturns and navigate the markets with confidence. successful hedging is about balancing risk and reward, a fundamental principle that underscores the strategic trading of options.

Psychological and Practical Considerations

The market is not just a reflection of economic indicators and corporate performance but also a mirror to the psychological state of its participants. The successful application of the iron condor strategy, or any options trading strategy for that matter, requires an in-depth understanding of one's psychological predispositions and biases.

1. Emotional Equilibrium: The ability to maintain emotional stability in the face of market fluctuations is crucial. Traders must develop the resilience to withstand the temptation to overreact to short-term market movements, adhering instead to their long-term strategy.

2. Cognitive Biases: Recognizing and mitigating cognitive biases such as overconfidence, confirmation bias, and loss aversion can significantly enhance decision-making processes. A trader prone to overconfidence may underestimate the risk inherent in an iron condor position, while one influenced by loss aversion might prematurely exit a profitable trade out of fear.

3. Stress Management: Effective stress management techniques are indispensable, as high levels of stress can cloud judgment and lead to irrational trading decisions. Regular physical exercise, meditation, and maintaining a healthy work-life balance are practices that can aid in managing stress.

Practical Wisdom for the Options Trader:

Beyond the psychological aspects, there are practical considerations that every trader must contend with to navigate the options market successfully.

1. Risk Assessment and Management: Understanding and managing risk is paramount. This involves not just the identification of potential risks but also the quantification and development of strategies to mitigate them. Diversification, setting stop-loss orders, and regularly reviewing and adjusting positions are practical steps traders can take to manage risk.

2. Market Research: Continuous market research is vital for staying informed about economic trends, company performance, and news events that could affect market conditions. This enables traders to adapt their strategies to changing market dynamics.

3. Record Keeping: Meticulous record-keeping allows traders to analyze their past transactions, learn from their successes and mistakes, and refine their strategies over time. A detailed trading journal should include the rationale behind trade decisions, the outcomes, and reflections on what was learned.

Case Study: Alex's Journey to Psychological Resilience:

Alex, a novice options trader, initially found himself overwhelmed by the volatility of the options market. He experienced a series of losses that led to self-doubt and a near-complete withdrawal from trading. Recognizing the need for a change, Alex began to focus on developing his psychological resilience. He took courses on cognitive biases, began practicing mindfulness to improve his emotional regulation, and started keeping a detailed trading journal. As he became more psychologically adept, his trading decisions improved, leading to more consistent results. Alex's journey underscores the critical importance of psychological resilience and practical wisdom in options trading.

The psychological and practical considerations of options trading are as complex as they are critical. Traders must cultivate a deep understanding of their psychological makeup and adopt a disciplined, practical approach to their trading activities. By doing so, they can navigate the landscapes of the market with greater confidence and efficacy, optimizing their use of the iron condor strategy and other sophisticated trading techniques. This blend of mental fortitude and pragmatic action is the hallmark of the seasoned options trader.

CHAPTER 6: PSYCHOLOGICAL AND PRACTICAL CONSIDERATIONS

Emotional discipline in trading is not merely about suppressing feelings of excitement or fear; it's about cultivating a mindset that prioritizes logic and strategy over instinct and impulse. To begin with, understanding the psychological triggers that lead to emotional trading is essential. These can range from the thrill of potential gains to the panic of unexpected downturns. Recognizing these triggers is the first step towards controlling them.

1. Establishing a Trading Plan: A well-defined trading plan, complete with entry and exit strategies, risk management techniques, and clear objectives, serves as a roadmap. It reduces the tendency to make impulsive decisions based on transient market movements or emotional reactions.

2. Setting Realistic Expectations: Unrealistic expectations can fuel greed and lead to excessive risk-taking. It's crucial for

traders to set achievable goals, based on thorough analysis and realistic assessment of market conditions.

3. Mindfulness and Self-Reflection: Incorporating mindfulness practices can enhance emotional regulation, helping traders to remain focused and calm. Regular self-reflection on one's trading decisions and the emotions that influenced them promotes a deeper understanding of personal biases and triggers.

The path of a trader is strewn with potential emotional pitfalls, from the fear of missing out (FOMO) on a seemingly lucrative opportunity, to the reluctance to cut losses, hoping against hope for a market reversal. Overcoming these pitfalls requires a disciplined approach:

- Developing Patience: Patience is a virtue nowhere more valued than in trading. Rushed decisions are often regretted ones. Cultivating patience helps in waiting for the right trading opportunities and avoiding the pitfalls of overtrading.

- Accepting Losses as Part of the Game: No trader wins every time. Accepting losses as an integral part of trading allows one to move on from them without emotional baggage, learning valuable lessons in the process.

- Staying Grounded in Volatility: Markets can change direction rapidly, and volatility can be unnerving. Staying grounded means keeping a long-term perspective, focusing on the trading plan, and not being swayed by short-term market fluctuations.

Consider the trader who, upon facing a loss, decides to "double down" instead of adhering to their stop-loss order, driven by the emotional need to "win back" the lost capital. More often than not, this leads to further losses. In contrast, the disciplined trader would accept the loss, analyze what went wrong, and refine their strategy, all without emotional turmoil influencing their decisions.

Emotional discipline in trading is not an innate skill but a cultivated practice. Through deliberate planning, realistic goal-setting, and continuous self-reflection, traders can fortify their emotional resilience. This not only helps in navigating the markets with a clear head but also in making decisions that align with long-term trading objectives. Remember, in trading, mastery over one's emotions is just as critical as mastery over market analysis and strategy.

Recognizing Emotional Traps

One of the most pervasive emotional traps is confirmation bias —the tendency to seek, interpret, and remember information that confirms pre-existing beliefs, while ignoring evidence to the contrary. In the throes of market analysis, a trader might become so fixated on their hypothesis that they overlook critical data pointing towards an opposing trend. The antidote? Cultivate a habit of actively seeking out dissenting viewpoints and data. Engaging with a diversity of opinions and analyses can mitigate the risk of falling prey to this bias.

Overconfidence, fueled by a string of successes, can lead traders to believe they possess an almost prophetic understanding of market movements. This hubris can lead to taking on excessive risk, neglecting the need for due diligence, and overriding the trading plan in favor of gut instincts. Recognizing overconfidence requires introspection and humility— acknowledging that no matter one's level of experience or past successes, the market remains unpredictable. Adherence to a disciplined trading strategy and risk management practices serves as a bulwark against the perils of overconfidence.

The pain of loss is psychologically twice as powerful as the pleasure of gain—a principle known as loss aversion. This fear can trap traders in unprofitable positions too long, in the hope of breaking even, or deter them from taking necessary risks. Recognizing loss aversion involves a candid assessment of one's risk tolerance and an understanding that losses are an inevitable aspect of trading. Setting predefined stop-loss orders and sticking to them can help traders escape the quicksand of loss aversion.

The gambler's fallacy is the erroneous belief that if something happens more frequently than normal during a given period, it will happen less frequently in the future, or vice versa. In trading, this fallacy can manifest in the belief that after a losing streak, a win is "due." The reality is that each trade is independent, and past outcomes do not influence future ones. Combatting this fallacy demands a firm grasp of probability and a steadfast commitment to statistical analysis over superstition.

Emotional contagion, the phenomenon of catching the emotions of others, can be especially potent in the high-stakes world of trading. The collective euphoria or panic of market participants can cloud individual judgment, leading to herd mentality. Recognizing emotional contagion involves maintaining a critical distance from market sentiment and relying on one's own analysis and convictions.

Navigating the trading landscape with emotional acuity requires vigilance and continuous self-awareness. By recognizing and understanding the emotional traps that lay in wait, traders can cultivate a mindset that prizes rationality over impulse, ensuring decisions are driven by strategy rather than emotion. In the domain of trading, where the heart often conflicts with the head, mastering one's emotional responses is not merely advantageous—it is essential.

Developing a Trading Plan and Sticking to It

1. Objective Setting: Begin with clarity—define what you wish to achieve through trading. Objectives should be S.M.A.R.T (Specific, Measurable, Achievable, Relevant, Time-bound). Whether it's achieving a certain return, learning new strategies, or supplementing income, clear objectives set the foundation.

2. Risk Management: This is the bulwark of your trading plan. Determine your risk tolerance level and adhere to it rigorously. This involves setting stop-loss orders, deciding on the percentage of capital to risk per trade, and understanding the risk-reward ratio. A golden rule is never to risk more than 1-2% of your trading capital on a single trade.

3. Market Analysis: Delve into the methodologies you will employ to analyze the market. Will it be technical analysis, fundamental analysis, or a combination of both? Define the indicators and tools you will utilize, such as moving averages, RSI, or economic reports, and articulate how these tools will guide your trading decisions.

4. Entry and Exit Criteria: Specify the conditions that must be met before you enter or exit a trade. This includes identifying buy and sell signals based on your market analysis and setting clear criteria for closing a position, whether in profit or loss.

5. Trading Diary: A key component that is often overlooked. Documenting each trade, including the rationale behind it, the outcomes, and reflections, can provide invaluable insights and facilitate continuous learning and strategy refinement.

6. Mental Rehearsal: Conditioning your mind through visualization techniques can fortify your resolve to stick to the plan. Imagine executing your plan under different market conditions, focusing on the process rather than the outcomes.

7. Regular Reviews: Schedule periodic reviews of your trading plan and diary. This is not merely an audit but an opportunity to recalibrate your strategies based on the evolving market and your personal growth as a trader.

8. Emotional Equilibrium: Developing techniques to manage emotions, such as mindfulness or meditation, can enhance your ability to adhere to your plan. Remember, the market is indifferent to emotions; it rewards discipline and penalizes impulsivity.

9. Support Network: Surround yourself with a community of traders. Sharing experiences, challenges, and strategies can offer fresh perspectives and reinforce your commitment to your trading discipline.

10. Continuous Education: The market is a perpetually evolving entity. Staying informed about market trends, financial news, and educational resources can bolster your confidence and commitment to your trading plan.

In trading, where uncertainty reigns and emotions can lead

astray, a trading plan stands as your lighthouse. It encapsulates your strategies, risk management principles, and personal goals. However, its true power is unlocked only through unwavering adherence. This commitment to your trading plan, coupled with continuous learning and emotional mastery, paves the path to not just surviving but thriving in the market's capricious landscape.

Importance of Taking Breaks and Reflective Practice

1. Cognitive Restoration: Research underscores the notion that short breaks can dramatically rejuvenate cognitive function, enhancing attention, creativity, and decision-making capabilities. In the milieu of trading, where decisions must be precise and analytical acuity is paramount, regular breaks can be the difference between profit and loss.

2. Stress Reduction: Trading is inherently stressful, with financial stakes high and market volatility a constant companion. Breaks serve as essential decompression periods, allowing the mind to relax, reset, and reduce cortisol levels, the body's primary stress hormone.

3. Avoiding Burnout: Chronic stress and continuous engagement without sufficient rest can lead to burnout—a state of emotional, physical, and mental exhaustion. By intentionally scheduling breaks, traders can safeguard against burnout, preserving their passion and drive for trading.

4. Insightful Reflections: Reflective practice involves a deliberate pause to contemplate one's actions, decisions, and the outcomes thereof. For traders, this means analyzing trades not just from a financial perspective but also examining the thought processes,

emotions, and biases that influenced those decisions.

5. Learning from Success and Failure: Reflective practice enables traders to dissect both successful and unsuccessful trades to identify patterns, strategies that worked, and mistakes to avoid. This holistic learning approach fosters a growth mindset, essential for continuous improvement.

6. Emotional Intelligence: Through reflection, traders develop greater emotional awareness and regulation. Recognizing the emotional triggers that lead to impulsive decisions can fortify a trader's resilience against the mercurial nature of the markets.

7. Scheduled Breaks: Integrate short, frequent breaks into your trading day, ensuring they are spent away from screens and market analysis to achieve genuine cognitive rest. Whether it's a brief walk, meditation, or a hobby, the activity should be rejuvenating.

8. Reflective Journaling: Maintain a reflective journal documenting not only your trades but also your emotional state, decision-making process, and reflections on both. This practice can illuminate patterns and areas for development.

9. Mindfulness and Meditation: These practices can enhance focus, reduce stress, and improve emotional regulation. Allocating time for mindfulness or meditation during breaks can amplify the restorative benefits.

10. Peer Discussions: Regularly engage with a community of traders to share experiences and reflections. These discussions can offer new insights, alternative perspectives, and mutual support.

11. Educational Breaks: Use some breaks to engage with educational content—books, webinars, or courses. This not only provides a break from the rigors of trading but also contributes to your continuous learning journey.

The demanding nature of trading necessitates a balanced approach, intertwining intense focus with deliberate periods of rest and reflection. Embracing the importance of taking breaks and engaging in reflective practice not only enhances a trader's performance but also contributes to their overall well-being and professional longevity. Through conscientious application of these practices, traders can cultivate a sustainable and enriching career in the ever-evolving dance of the markets.

Record Keeping and Analysis

1. Comprehensive Documentation: effective record keeping involves the detailed documentation of each trade, including date, time, underlying asset, position size, strike prices, premiums received or paid, and any commissions or fees. However, it transcends mere financial transactions to include contextual factors such as market conditions, prevailing volatility, and the trader's rationale behind entering and exiting the trade.

2. Digital Tools and Platforms: While traditional ledger books once served traders well, the digital age offers sophisticated software and platforms designed for trade documentation. These tools can automate data entry for efficiency and accuracy, and they often come equipped with analytical capabilities to derive insights from the amassed data.

3. Regular Reviews: The act of keeping records is rendered futile without regular and deliberate review sessions. These sessions serve as opportunities not just to tally wins and losses but to engage deeply with the data, discern patterns, and identify strategies that yield consistent success or reveal areas of recurrent failure.

4. Performance Metrics: Analysis begins with quantifying performance through metrics such as win/loss ratio, average profit per winning trade versus average loss per losing trade, and overall profitability. Advanced metrics might include measures of risk-adjusted return like the Sharpe ratio, which evaluates performance relative to the volatility endured to achieve those returns.

5. Strategic Insights: Beyond raw performance, analysis seeks to unearth strategic insights. This involves dissecting trades based on various factors—such as time to expiration, distance of strike prices from the underlying asset's price, or specific market conditions—to determine what configurations and circumstances tend to favor the iron condor strategy.

6. Behavioral Analysis: An often-overlooked dimension is the trader's behavior and decision-making process. By reviewing records with an eye toward the psychological and emotional states influencing trade decisions, traders can become more aware of biases (such as overconfidence or aversion to loss) that might skew their strategies.

7. Strategy Adjustment: Armed with analytical insights, traders are better positioned to refine their strategies. This might involve adjusting strike price selections, tightening or widening spreads based on volatility analysis, or reevaluating entry and

exit criteria.

8. Risk Management Enhancements: Analysis often highlights areas where risk management can be tightened. This could result in adjusting position sizes, employing stop-loss orders more strategically, or diversifying trade allocations across different assets or time frames.

9. Psychological Conditioning: Understanding the emotional and psychological patterns that emerge from trade analysis can lead to better emotional regulation, helping traders stay disciplined and focused on strategy rather than reacting impulsively to market movements.

The disciplines of record keeping and analysis are not merely administrative tasks but are integral to the fabric of successful trading. They provide the clarity, insight, and evidence needed to navigate the complexities of the market with informed confidence. For those wielding the iron condor strategy, these practices are indispensable tools in the quest for strategic mastery and profitability. Through diligent documentation and insightful analysis, traders can sculpt a path of continuous improvement, adapting and thriving amidst the ever-changing dynamics of the financial markets.

What to Track in Your Trading Journal

The trading journal stands as a beacon of self-reflection, strategy refinement, and disciplined commitment. This essential tool transcends mere record-keeping; it's a repository of learning and a mirror reflecting a trader's journey through the tumultuous markets. Within the context of iron condor trading, the journal's role assumes even greater significance, offering insights into the nuanced strategies and decisions shaping a trader's success.

1. Trade Logistics: Begin with the basics—document the date, time, underlying asset, position (buy/sell), quantity, strike prices for both the call and put options, premiums received or paid, and the expiration date. Include transaction costs and any applicable fees to accurately reflect the financial outcome of the trade.

2. Market Context: Capture the broader market context at the time of the trade. Note the prevailing market trends, significant economic announcements, or geopolitical events that could influence market sentiment and volatility. This snapshot of market conditions serves as a critical reference for evaluating the trade's performance in its specific context.

3. Risk Assessment and Management Strategies: Detail the risk management strategies employed, including the rationale behind the size of the position and any adjustments made (or considered) in response to market movements. Include notes on stop-loss orders, if used, and how decisions were made to either adjust the trade or let it run its course.

4. Emotional and Psychological Notes: Trading is as much a psychological endeavor as it is strategic. Record your emotional state and confidence level in the strategy at both the entry and exit points. Reflect on any moments of hesitation, second-guessing, or impulse decisions to identify emotional patterns that could affect trading decisions.

5. Outcome and Review: After the trade has reached its conclusion, whether it was closed manually or expired,

document the outcome. Include both the financial result and a review of the trade's execution against the initial plan. This reflective practice is crucial for identifying both successful decisions and areas needing improvement.

6. Identify Patterns: Over time, your journal will reveal patterns in both market behavior and personal trading tendencies. These insights are invaluable for refining your strategy, improving decision-making processes, and understanding your risk tolerance.

7. Strategic Refinement: Use your journal to test and refine different strategies under various market conditions. It becomes a laboratory for experimentation, where lessons learned lead to strategic innovation.

8. Emotional Regulation: By consistently tracking emotional states and their impact on trading decisions, traders can develop greater emotional discipline. This awareness fosters a more methodical approach to trading, reducing the influence of emotional volatility on strategic execution.

Your trading journal is much more than a ledger; it's the narrative of your journey through the complex world of options trading. It holds the key to unlocking deeper insights into market dynamics, personal biases, and the efficacy of trading strategies. For the iron condor trader, it provides a structured mechanism for continuous learning and strategic evolution, ensuring that each trade, regardless of its outcome, contributes to a broader understanding of the markets and oneself. Through diligent tracking and reflective analysis, the trading journal becomes an indispensable ally on the path to trading mastery.

Analyzing Trades: The Good, the Bad, the Ugly

The analytical dissection of past trades—categorizing them as the good, the bad, and the ugly—represents a cornerstone practice for the astute options trader. Such retrospective examination not only crystallizes lessons learned but also paves the way for the refinement of strategies, especially in iron condor trading. Each category, with its distinct characteristics, offers unique insights and learning opportunities, thus contributing to the trader's evolution.

1. Well-timed Entries and Exits: Analyze trades where the timing was near impeccable—entering when the market's volatility was optimal and exiting either at predetermined profit targets or just before an unfavorable movement. Document the market conditions and the decision-making process that led to such precise timing.

2. Robust Risk Management: Highlight trades where risk management protocols were followed rigorously, resulting in minimized losses or safeguarded profits. Assess the effectiveness of stop-loss levels, position sizing, and any adjustments made to respond to market dynamics.

3. Accurate Market Prediction: Examine instances where your market analysis was spot-on, leading to profitable trades. Identify the tools, indicators, and information sources that contributed to accurate market readings.

4. Misjudged Market Conditions: Reflect on trades that went awry due to a misinterpretation of market conditions or overlooked signals. Scrutinize the analysis techniques used and

consider alternative approaches that might have yielded a more accurate assessment.

5. Overlooked Risk Management: Identify trades where lapses in risk management led to unnecessary losses. Analyze the oversight—was it due to complacency, a misunderstanding of the trade's risk profile, or perhaps an underestimation of market volatility?

6. Faulty Strategy Implementation: Examine trades where the strategy was sound in theory but faltered in execution. Investigate whether the flaw lay in the trade setup, timing, or perhaps a misalignment of the strategy with market conditions.

7. Severe Misjudgments: Delve into trades that resulted in substantial losses, often due to a combination of errors, emotional decision-making, or extreme market events. These trades serve as stark reminders of the importance of humility, continuous learning, and the need for an ever-vigilant approach to risk management.

8. Psychological Pitfalls: Unpack instances where psychological biases—overconfidence, fear of missing out (FOMO), or the inability to accept a loss—led to disastrous trade decisions. Reflecting on these can fortify emotional discipline and enhance decision-making processes.

9. External Factors: Sometimes, an 'ugly' trade results from unforeseeable events—geopolitical developments, sudden economic downturns, or other black swan events. While not always avoidable, analyzing these instances can highlight the importance of hedging strategies and maintaining a diversified portfolio.

The process of analyzing the good, the bad, and the ugly necessitates a disciplined, objective, and reflective mindset. It's not merely about celebrating triumphs or lamenting losses but about extracting actionable insights to sculpt a more informed, resilient, and adaptive trading strategy. For the iron condor trader, this practice is invaluable. It fosters a deeper understanding of market mechanisms, enhances risk management skills, and ultimately, hones the trader's ability to navigate the complexities of the options market with greater confidence and proficiency.

Maintaining a meticulous, analytical approach to reviewing past trades, traders can transform even the most disheartening losses into powerful learning experiences. It's through the continuous cycle of action, analysis, and adjustment that mastery in the art of iron condor trading is achieved, setting the foundation for sustained success in the dynamic world of options trading.

Improving Your Strategy Based on Historical Performance

Elevating your trading strategy by scrutinizing historical performance is akin to an alchemist refining metals into gold. The process is , demanding a keen eye for detail, a rigorous analytical approach, and an unwavering commitment to improvement. For traders, particularly those navigating the nuanced landscape of iron condors, the historical performance of their trades is a treasure trove of insights, waiting to be deciphered and utilized for future prosperity.

1. Comprehensive Trade Log: Begin with the meticulous maintenance of a trade log, detailing every trade executed, including the strategy employed, entry and exit points, market

conditions, and the outcome. This log serves as the raw data for all future analysis.

2. Performance Metrics: Extract key performance metrics from the trade log, such as win/loss ratio, average profit/loss per trade, maximum drawdown, and Sharpe ratio. These metrics provide a quantitative foundation for evaluating the strategy's effectiveness.

3. Behavioral Analysis: Incorporate notes on your emotional and psychological state for each trade. Did emotions influence decision-making? This qualitative data is crucial for identifying patterns that might skew strategic decisions.

4. Win/Loss Pattern Analysis: Look for patterns in wins and losses. Are successful trades clustered around specific market conditions or times of the year? Such patterns can guide future strategy adjustments.

5. Strategy Comparison: If multiple strategies are in use, compare their performance under similar conditions. This can highlight which strategies are more effective and under what circumstances.

6. Risk-Reward Assessment: Re-assess the risk-reward ratio of past trades. Were the losses due to taking too high a risk for the potential reward? Adjusting this ratio can significantly improve future strategy performance.

7. Market Condition Sensitivity: Adjust your strategy based on the sensitivity to different market conditions. If your historical performance shows better results in low volatility environments, tailor your strategy to capitalize on these

conditions.

8. Entry and Exit Refinement: Use historical data to fine-tune your entry and exit criteria. Perhaps entering trades earlier in the trend or extending the holding period could enhance results.

9. Risk Management Reinforcement: Strengthen risk management tactics based on past shortcomings. This might involve setting tighter stop-loss orders, adjusting position sizes, or diversifying across different assets.

10. Test Adjustments: Before fully integrating changes into your live trading strategy, test them through paper trading or backtesting against historical data. This provides an initial assessment of the adjustments' efficacy without risking capital.

11. Phased Implementation: Gradually implement successful adjustments into your live trading strategy. This phased approach allows for real-time evaluation and further refinement.

12. Continuous Feedback Loop: Establish a continuous feedback loop where ongoing performance data is analyzed and used to make further adjustments. This iterative process ensures that the strategy remains dynamic and adaptable to changing market conditions.

Improving your strategy based on historical performance is not a one-off task but a continuous journey of self-improvement and learning. It demands resilience, adaptability, and an unwavering commitment to excellence. By embracing this journey, traders can transcend the confines of past performances, evolving into more proficient, strategic, and successful market navigators.

the meticulous analysis of historical performance and the strategic adjustments that follow are not merely exercises in data analysis; they are rites of passage that every trader must undergo to achieve mastery in the complex yet rewarding world of iron condor trading. Through this process, traders not only improve their strategies but also foster a deeper understanding of the markets, their own psychological predispositions, and the art of trading itself.

Learning from Mistakes

In options trading, where the iron condor spreads its wings wide across the spectrum of risk and reward, learning from mistakes is not just advisable; it is imperative for survival and success. Each misstep, while potentially costly, is a cornerstone for building a more robust strategy. It is through the careful dissection of errors that traders can sculpt their path to mastery.

1. Error Logging: Integral to learning from mistakes is the practice of maintaining an error log. This log should detail not just the financial loss incurred but also the decision-making process that led to the mistake, market conditions, and the emotional state of the trader at the time. This comprehensive approach turns each error into a lesson waiting to be learned.

2. Common Pitfalls: Identify and categorize common mistakes, such as misinterpreting market signals, emotional trading (greed or fear), overleveraging, ignoring risk management principles, and underestimating market volatility. Recognizing patterns in errors can lead to systemic improvements in trading strategy.

3. Consultation and Reflection: Leverage the collective wisdom of the trading community by sharing your mistakes in trading forums or with a mentor. Often, external perspectives can offer insights that are not apparent from a first-person viewpoint. Reflect deeply on the feedback received and integrate it into your approach.

4. Emotional Discipline: One of the most frequent sources of error is emotional decision-making. Implementing techniques such as meditation, journaling, and strict adherence to a trading plan can fortify emotional resilience, reducing the likelihood of repeat mistakes.

5. Risk Management Overhaul: Mistakes often stem from inadequate or failed risk management strategies. Reevaluate your approach to position sizing, stop-loss orders, and diversification. Consider adopting more sophisticated risk management techniques, such as using delta-neutral positions to hedge against market moves.

6. Strategy Refinement: Use the specific insights gained from your mistakes to refine your trading strategy. This could involve adjusting your criteria for selecting strike prices and expiration dates, or it might mean a more fundamental shift in the way you identify suitable market conditions for iron condor trades.

7. Paper Trading Revisions: Before applying lessons learned from your mistakes to your live trading strategy, engage in a period of paper trading. This simulated environment provides a risk-free space to validate the effectiveness of your adjustments.

8. Incremental Live Testing: Gradually incorporate successful

strategies from paper trading into your live trading, starting with smaller positions. This measured approach allows you to fine-tune adjustments in real-world conditions without exposing yourself to undue risk.

9. The Virtue of Patience: Embrace patience as both a strategic principle and a psychological discipline. The eagerness to recoup losses can lead to a repetition of past mistakes. Allowing ample time for your adjustments to prove their worth is crucial.

Learning from mistakes in iron condor trading, or any form of options trading, is a continuous cycle of evolution. It requires an unyielding commitment to self-assessment, the humility to acknowledge errors, and the courage to change course. By transforming mistakes into stepping stones, traders can elevate their practice from mere participation in the markets to achieving true proficiency and, ultimately, mastery.

Through this iterative process of reflection, adjustment, and experimentation, traders not only sharpen their skill set but also deepen their understanding of the market's complex dynamics. Mistakes, in this light, are not merely setbacks but invaluable lessons that pave the way for future success.

Common Pitfalls in Iron Condor Trading

Iron condor trading, with its allure of high probability winning trades and premium income generation, is not without its pitfalls. These common traps can ensnare novice and experienced traders alike, leading to unexpected losses and frustration. By identifying these pitfalls, we position ourselves to navigate around them, refining our trading approach for better outcomes.

1. Misplaced Trust in Historical Success: A common mistake is the belief that a strategy that worked well in the past will continue to do so under all future market conditions. Iron condors thrive in stable, range-bound markets, but can suffer during unexpected volatility spikes. Traders must remain adaptable, recognizing that strategy adjustments might be necessary as market dynamics evolve.

2. Underestimation of Tail Risks: The iron condor strategy relies on selling options with a low probability of expiring in-the-money. However, this approach can lead to complacency about the risk of significant loss from rare but extreme market movements, known as "tail risks." Proper risk management must account for these potential outliers.

3. Failure to Plan for Adjustments: Successful iron condor trading requires not just a setup plan but also a pre-defined adjustment strategy for when market conditions change unfavorably. Lack of an adjustment plan can lead to panicked decision-making in the heat of the moment.

4. Rigidity in Adjustment Execution: Even with an adjustment strategy in place, some traders fail to execute adjustments due to emotional attachment to their original position or hope that the market will revert. Timely and decisive action is paramount.

5. Ignoring Account Size Limitations: A frequent oversight is the failure to match trade size with account size, leading to overexposure. Each iron condor trade should only represent a small fraction of one's total trading capital to mitigate risk effectively.

6. Neglect of Diversification: Some traders place multiple iron condor trades on highly correlated assets, mistakenly believing they are diversified. True diversification involves spreading trades across uncorrelated assets to reduce systemic risk.

7. Chasing Losses: After a losing trade, the urge to quickly recoup losses can drive traders to make impulsive, higher-risk trades. This gamble rarely pays off and can lead to further losses.

8. Overtrading: The relative ease of setting up iron condor trades can lead to overtrading, as traders seek to generate more premium income. However, this can significantly increase exposure to risk, particularly during volatile market conditions.

9. Selection of Inappropriate Strike Prices: Choosing strike prices too close to the current market price for the sake of higher premiums increases the risk of the options being exercised. Strike selection must balance premium income against the probability of the option expiring worthless.

10. Misjudgement of Expiration Dates: Opting for longer expiration periods can increase premium income but also amplifies the exposure to price movement. Conversely, very short expirations reduce the window for adjustment if the market moves unfavorably.

Recognizing and avoiding these pitfalls requires a blend of discipline, continuous learning, and an adaptive mindset. Incorporating a thorough risk assessment, having clear criteria for trade selection and adjustment, and fostering psychological resilience against the lure of quick profits are foundational elements of successful iron condor trading.

Understanding these common mistakes and implementing strategies to avoid them, traders can enhance their performance in the options market. The goal is not to achieve perfection but to cultivate a trading practice that is resilient, adaptable, and grounded in sound risk management principles.

How to Analyze and Learn from Lost Trades

1. Comprehensive Trade Documentation: The foundation for learning from lost trades is a comprehensive trading journal. This should include not just the numbers, but also the rationale behind trade decisions, market conditions, expected outcomes, and psychological state. Such detailed records make it possible to review trades with the benefit of hindsight, identifying where expectations diverged from reality.

2. Objective Performance Review: Analyze each lost trade without bias, focusing on the data and facts. Assess the trade setup, execution, and the sequence of market events leading to the loss. The goal is to pinpoint the moment or decision that initiated the path to an unfavorable outcome.

3. Recurrent Errors: Look for patterns that may indicate a recurring mistake or oversight. Common issues include misreading market signals, consistently choosing suboptimal strike prices, or failing to adjust to changing market conditions in a timely manner.

4. Market Condition Misinterpretation: Identify any misinterpretations of market conditions or volatility that contributed to the loss. Understanding the market context in which certain strategies falter is crucial for refining trade

selection and adjustment strategies.

5. Emotional Triggers: Reflect on the emotional state before, during, and after the trade. Emotional decisions can cloud judgment, leading to premature exits from positions or failure to execute planned adjustments. Identifying emotional triggers helps in developing strategies to maintain discipline in future trades.

6. Bias Recognition: Acknowledge any cognitive biases at play, such as confirmation bias, which may lead to disregarding contradictory market information. Recognizing these biases is the first step in mitigating their influence on decision-making.

7. Strategy Refinement: Based on the analysis, identify specific aspects of the trading strategy that require adjustment. This might involve modifying criteria for trade entry, adjustment, or exit, as well as reevaluating the selection of underlying assets or expiration periods.

8. Risk Management Enhancement: Assess whether the loss was exacerbated by inadequate risk management practices. Consider adjustments to position sizing, diversification strategies, or the implementation of more stringent stop-loss criteria.

9. Actionable Insights: Convert the insights gained from the analysis into actionable steps. This could include changes to the trading plan, adjustment strategies, or risk management guidelines.

10. Commitment to Continuous Improvement: Embrace the mindset of continuous learning. The options market is dynamic, and strategies must evolve to remain effective. Regularly

scheduled reviews of both successful and unsuccessful trades are essential for ongoing development.

Analyzing and learning from lost trades is not merely about avoiding future losses; it's about evolving as a trader. It involves developing an in-depth understanding of the markets, refining trading strategies, enhancing emotional discipline, and strengthening risk management practices. By systematically reviewing lost trades, traders can extract valuable lessons, turning setbacks into stepping stones towards trading mastery.

Cultivating a Growth Mindset

1. Challenges as Opportunities: The first step toward cultivating a growth mindset is reframing how we perceive challenges. In the context of iron condor trading, each new trade presents a unique set of variables—market conditions, volatility, and the economic landscape. Viewing these challenges as opportunities to apply and extend our expertise is crucial. It involves shifting from a mindset that dreads potential failure to one that eagerly anticipates the learning that each trade, regardless of its outcome, will bring.

2. The Iron Condor as a Learning Laboratory: Given its structure, trading an iron condor requires a deep understanding of options pricing, volatility, and market sentiment. Each trade becomes a mini-experiment, providing real-world feedback on our hypotheses and strategies. By approaching each trade as a learning opportunity, traders can detach their ego from the outcome, focusing instead on the accumulation of knowledge and experience.

3. Effort over Innate Ability: A foundational aspect of the growth

mindset is the belief that effort is a key driver of success. In trading, as in learning any complex skill, sustained effort over time leads to mastery. This means dedicating time to analyze markets, study historical volatility patterns, and simulate trade outcomes. It's about recognizing that proficiency in trading iron condors comes through persistent study and practice, not innate talent.

4. Incremental Progress: Progress in options trading, especially with strategies as sophisticated as the iron condor, is often incremental. Valuing and acknowledging these small gains is crucial. It could be improving the accuracy of volatility forecasts, fine-tuning risk management techniques, or simply becoming more disciplined in trade journaling. Celebrating these incremental improvements reinforces the value of effort and supports the continuation of the learning journey.

5. Setbacks as Feedback: A growth mindset interprets setbacks not as evidence of incapacity but as valuable feedback. In iron condor trading, losses are inevitable. However, each loss carries with it data—information about market behavior, the effectiveness of our strategy under specific conditions, and our own psychological responses to stress and uncertainty. Analyzing this data helps refine our approach, making us better traders.

6. Systematic Reflection: Cultivating a growth mindset involves developing a systematic process for reflecting on both successful and unsuccessful trades. This could include reviewing trade logs, discussing outcomes with a mentor or peer group, and even using simulation software to replay trade scenarios. The key is to extract actionable insights from each reflection, applying these lessons to future trades.

Cultivating a growth mindset is a dynamic and ongoing process. It requires commitment, reflection, and the willingness to engage deeply with both the successes and challenges inherent in iron condor trading. By embracing challenges, valuing effort, and learning from setbacks, traders can develop a resilient and adaptive approach to the markets. This mindset not only enhances trading performance but also contributes to personal growth and fulfillment, extending well beyond the trading desk.

Case Studies of Successful Iron Condor Trades

1

Background: Amid the quarterly earnings season, a seasoned trader, Alex, recognized an opportunity in the stock of a leading tech company. Known for its minimal earnings-related volatility but steady growth, the company was a prime candidate for an iron condor strategy.

Strategic Execution: Alex meticulously selected strike prices that were out of the money (OTM) for both the call and put spreads, ensuring a wide enough range to account for any unexpected movements. The chosen expiration was closely post-earnings announcement, leveraging the typical drop in implied volatility post-earnings.

Outcome: The stock moved within the expected range, and as the implied volatility dropped, the value of the iron condor position decreased rapidly, allowing Alex to close out the position for a substantial profit three days post-earnings.

Lessons Learned: This trade underscored the importance of understanding historical volatility patterns around earnings announcements and selecting strike prices that provide a sufficient buffer while still offering attractive premiums.

2

Background: During the tumultuous period leading up to a critical Brexit vote, many traders avoided the market due to the high uncertainty and volatility. However, Jordan, a contrarian trader, saw this as a perfect setup for an iron condor.

Strategic Execution: Jordan chose index options that represented the European market, expecting that the actual move would be less extreme than the implied volatility suggested. The strike prices were selected to create a wide profitability range, with expirations set for one month post-vote.

Outcome: The market did experience volatility spikes on the vote's announcement but eventually settled within Jordan's predicted range. The inflated premiums collected upfront due to the high implied volatility pre-vote provided a cushion that helped maintain profitability.

Lessons Learned: This trade highlighted the efficacy of iron condors in leveraging market overreactions. The key takeaway was the value of a wide range to absorb significant moves and the advantage of entering trades when implied volatility is at a peak.

3

Background: Facing a stagnant period in equity markets, trader Mia turned her attention to commodities – specifically, oil. With tensions rising in the Middle East but no immediate threats to supply, implied volatility in oil futures spiked.

Strategic Execution: Mia applied an iron condor to an ETF tracking oil prices, betting that actual volatility would remain low. She carefully chose her strike prices to account for possible geopolitical escalations, setting a broader range than usual.

Outcome: Despite brief spikes in oil prices due to geopolitical rhetoric, the overall supply and demand kept prices within Mia's range, leading to a profitable trade as the premiums on both sides of the condor eroded with time.

Lessons Learned: This case study demonstrated the iron condor's versatility beyond equities, showing its potential in commodity markets where fundamental factors can provide a predictable range despite geopolitical fear-induced volatility.

These case studies of successful iron condor trades illuminate several core principles of this strategy. First, a deep understanding of the underlying asset's volatility pattern is crucial. Second, selecting appropriate strike prices and expirations can significantly enhance the trade's probability of success. Lastly, external market events, whether earnings announcements, geopolitical developments, or economic referendums, can serve as catalysts for iron condor opportunities, provided the trader maintains a disciplined approach to risk management.

Through these narratives, we grasp not just the mechanics but the artistry behind successful iron condor trading. Each trade tells a story of anticipation, strategy, and adaptability, offering valuable lessons for traders at every level of expertise.

CHAPTER 7: CASE STUDIES OF SUCCESSFUL IRON CONDOR TRADES

E conomic indicators are akin to the vital signs of the market, offering insights into its health and direction. Traders must become adept at reading these signs, from the gross domestic product (GDP) growth rates and employment figures to inflation data and interest rate decisions by central banks. Each of these indicators can sway the market, affecting asset prices and, consequently, the optimal setup for an iron condor trade.

Beyond economic fundamentals, technical analysis provides traders with tools to forecast market movements based on past price actions and volume data. This involves identifying patterns and trends in market charts, which can signal potential entry and exit points for trades. For the iron condor strategist, understanding support and resistance levels, as well as recognizing bullish or bearish chart formations, is paramount in choosing the right strike prices and expiration dates.

The market is not solely driven by cold, hard data; it is also a creature of sentiment and perception. Sentiment analysis, therefore, becomes a crucial aspect of market condition analysis. This involves gauging the mood of the market participants, from the retail investor to the institutional behemoth. Are traders bullish, expecting prices to rise, or bearish, anticipating a downturn? Tools such as the Volatility Index (VIX), news headlines, and social media trends offer a window into the market's soul, allowing the iron condor trader to align their strategy with the prevailing emotional currents.

In today's interconnected world, a ripple in one part of the globe can turn into a wave by the time it reaches another. Geopolitical events, natural disasters, and significant policy changes can have profound effects on market conditions. The astute trader must keep an ear to the ground, ready to adjust their iron condor positions in response to these external shocks. This requires not only a keen awareness of current events but also an understanding of their potential impacts on various sectors and asset classes.

With a comprehensive analysis of market conditions in hand, the trader is well-equipped to deploy the iron condor strategy effectively. In stable, low-volatility markets, a classic iron condor setup may suffice. However, in times of uncertainty or high volatility, adjustments may be necessary, such as tightening or widening the wings of the condor to manage risk and potential returns.

The Artful Navigator

In options trading, the pre-trade market analysis emerges as the lighthouse guiding traders through the mist. This pivotal process, akin to a ritual performed with both reverence and precision, sets the stage for the deployment of the iron condor strategy. It is here, in the quiet before the storm of market open, that traders arm themselves with knowledge, strategy, and foresight.

The foundation of pre-trade market analysis is built upon a thorough review of both macroeconomic indicators and microeconomic details. This dual focus ensures that traders are not blindsided by larger economic trends while they fine-tune their strategies for specific trades. Macroeconomic analysis might include reviewing global economic reports, geopolitical tensions, and upcoming announcements from central banks, which can sway market sentiment and volatility levels—critical factors for timing an iron condor trade.

Microeconomic analysis, on the other hand, delves into the specifics of the chosen underlying asset. For options traders, this means understanding the business model of the company, its sector's health, and any upcoming earnings reports or product launches that could significantly impact stock price and, by extension, options volatility.

Technical Analysis Deep Dive

While the previous section on analyzing market conditions introduced the importance of technical analysis, the pre-trade phase demands a deeper engagement with this discipline. Traders meticulously chart the historical performance of their chosen asset, identifying patterns that could indicate future movements. Tools like moving averages, Bollinger Bands, and the Relative Strength Index (RSI) become invaluable in assessing whether the asset is currently overbought or oversold—a crucial consideration for timing entry and exit points for iron condor positions.

Understanding the prevailing sentiment towards the chosen asset adds another layer of depth to the pre-trade analysis. This involves a granular approach to news consumption, social media monitoring, and analyzing investor sentiment indicators. Special attention is paid to the implied volatility of options, which serves as a direct gauge of market sentiment towards the underlying asset. A spike in implied volatility could suggest that the market is anticipating significant price movement, which might necessitate adjustments to the iron condor strategy.

Armed with comprehensive market data, the savvy trader now engages in scenario planning. This involves asking "what-if" questions and preparing for multiple market scenarios. What if the earnings report exceeds market expectations? What if geopolitical tensions escalate? For each scenario, the trader evaluates the potential impact on the underlying asset's price and the broader market's volatility. This exercise not only aids in fine-tuning the iron condor setup but also in developing contingency plans for active position management.

With the pre-trade market analysis complete, the trader is now poised to finalize their iron condor strategy. This includes selecting the optimal strike prices, expiration dates, and position sizes based on the analysis conducted. Risk management parameters are set, including predefined exit points and stop-loss orders, to protect against unforeseen market movements.

The Convergence of Analysis and Action

The premise of an iron condor strategy is predicated on the

underlying asset's price remaining within a specific range. However, financial markets are notoriously unpredictable, influenced by a myriad of factors that can cause sudden and significant price movements. It is in these moments that the iron condor trader must be most vigilant, ready to make adjustments to mitigate losses or capture unforeseen gains.

Adjustment triggers can be broadly categorized into market-driven and strategy-driven. Market-driven triggers include significant economic announcements, unexpected geopolitical events, or sudden shifts in investor sentiment that lead to increased volatility. Strategy-driven triggers, on the other hand, are related to the specifics of the iron condor setup—such as the price of the underlying asset approaching the short strike price, or an unforeseen change in implied volatility affecting the value of the options positions.

Adjustment Techniques: A Tactical Overview

Once a trigger for adjustment has been identified, the trader must decide on the most appropriate adjustment technique. These can include:

- Rolling Out: This involves closing the current position and opening a new one with a later expiration date. This technique is particularly useful if the trader believes that the underlying asset will return to its expected range given more time.

- Rolling Up/Down: If one side of the iron condor is threatened (the call spread in a bullish move, or the put spread in a bearish move), the trader may choose to close the threatened side and reopen it at a higher or lower strike price. This adjusts the range in which the asset can fluctuate profitably but also impacts the potential profit and loss.

- Adding Spreads: In certain scenarios, adding another iron condor at different strike prices can help balance the position and capitalize on increased volatility. This increases complexity and requires a keen understanding of how the added spreads interact with the original position.

In-trade adjustments are not merely technical maneuvers; they are also psychological challenges. The decision to adjust a trade can be fraught with hesitation, second-guessing, and the emotional weight of potential loss. The successful trader, however, learns to approach these decisions with a calculated mindset, guided by strategy and risk management principles rather than emotion.

The modern trader has at their disposal a suite of real-time data analytics tools that can provide invaluable insights into market trends, volatility fluctuations, and potential price movements. Leveraging these tools can provide the empirical basis needed to make informed adjustment decisions.

Case Study: A Tactical Pivot

Consider a scenario where a trader has set up an iron condor on a tech stock ahead of its quarterly earnings report, anticipating low volatility. Unexpectedly, the company announces a groundbreaking new product, causing the stock to surge towards the upper strike price. Recognizing the trigger, the trader promptly rolls up the call spread, adjusting the range to accommodate the new market reality. This decision, made swiftly and strategically, mitigates potential losses and preserves the integrity of the iron condor strategy.

In-trade adjustment decisions are the crucible in which the iron condor strategy is tested and refined. They require a blend of vigilance, strategic foresight, and the courage to act under pressure. By mastering the art of in-trade adjustments, the trader not only safeguards their position but also seizes opportunities for profit in the ever-changing market landscape.

Post-trade Review

After the storm of market fluctuations and the adrenaline of in-trade adjustments comes the calm and introspection of post-trade review. This essential phase in the iron condor strategy's lifecycle transcends mere analysis; it is a conduit for growth, learning, and refinement. Each trade, whether it culminates in profit or loss, carries with it valuable lessons that, when properly dissected, can illuminate the path to enhanced trading acumen.

The post-trade review process begins with establishing a structured framework that encompasses both quantitative metrics and qualitative insights. This dual-lens approach ensures a comprehensive understanding of the trade's outcome. The quantitative analysis might include metrics such as the return on investment, maximum potential gain versus actual gain, and the efficiency of the in-trade adjustments. Qualitatively, the review seeks to capture the trader's rationale behind each decision, the emotional and psychological dynamics at play, and the external factors influencing the trade.

Here, the trader delves into the numerical data, comparing initial projections with actual outcomes. This involves a meticulous examination of how close the trade came to hitting its maximum profit or loss thresholds and the impact of any adjustments made. Tools and software that offer advanced analytics and visualization can greatly aid this process, allowing for a deeper dive into performance metrics.

Qualitative Analysis: The Story Behind the Numbers

Beyond the cold hard numbers lies the narrative of the trade. This part of the review process is introspective, focusing on the trader's thought process, strategy adherence, and reaction to market developments. Key questions to explore include:

- What was the initial rationale for choosing this particular iron condor setup?

- Were there any unforeseen market events that influenced the trade? How was the response to these events?

- Did emotional biases or psychological factors sway any trading decisions?

- How effective were the in-trade adjustments? Could a different strategy have yielded a better outcome?

Learning from Mistakes and Successes

The essence of the post-trade review lies in its capacity to turn experience into actionable knowledge. Mistakes are dissected to prevent future repetition, while successful strategies are cataloged for future application. This iterative learning process is crucial for the evolution of a trader's skill set and strategy toolkit.

Case Study: Reflections on a Missed Opportunity

Imagine a scenario where a trader, after adjusting an iron condor position due to an unexpected market rally, fails to achieve the anticipated profit due to a late execution of the adjustment. The post-trade review reveals that the delay was partly due to over-analysis and partly due to a hesitance to accept a smaller profit than initially projected. The qualitative analysis uncovers a tendency towards perfectionism and a fear of making wrong decisions, which, when combined with the quantitative analysis, suggests areas for psychological and strategic improvement.

The final step in the post-trade review process is the integration of learned lessons into future trading endeavors. This might involve refining the criteria for adjustment triggers, enhancing the use of real-time data analytics, or working on psychological resilience and decision-making under pressure.

The post-trade review is not an endpoint but a vital component of a continuous cycle of improvement. By approaching each review with honesty, curiosity, and a commitment to growth, traders can elevate their mastery of the iron condor strategy. This process, when consistently applied, not only enhances profitability but also contributes to the trader's development as a disciplined, reflective, and adaptive market participant.

Detailed Breakdown of Trade Execution

Before the execution phase, thorough preparation is crucial. This involves a detailed analysis of market conditions, including volatility levels, economic indicators, and upcoming events that might impact the underlying asset. Tools such as volatility indexes and economic calendars become invaluable in this stage, providing a backdrop against which the iron condor strategy is framed.

The choice of the underlying asset is the first critical decision. It should be characterized by high liquidity, ensuring that options contracts can be bought and sold with minimal slippage, and a stable price action that aligns with the neutral outlook of the iron condor strategy. Indices often serve as ideal candidates due to their inherent stability and liquidity.

With the underlying asset in focus, the next step involves selecting strike prices for the call and put spreads. This decision is guided by a comprehensive analysis of the asset's historical price movements, current market sentiment, and projected future trends. The expiry date is chosen to balance the trade-off between time decay (theta) and the chance of the underlying asset's price breaching the strike prices. Typically, a period of 30 to 60 days until expiration is favored to optimize theta decay while providing sufficient time for the trade to unfold as anticipated.

The execution phase is where precision is paramount. The trader initiates the trade by simultaneously selling an out-of-the-money (OTM) call spread and an OTM put spread. This involves selling a call option and buying a higher strike call option (forming the call spread) and selling a put option and buying a lower strike put option (forming the put spread). The sequence of these transactions can significantly impact the entry price; hence, some traders prefer to execute each spread as a single transaction to mitigate price movement risks.

Once the trade is in place, continuous monitoring is essential.

Market conditions can change rapidly, and the iron condor strategy may require adjustments to manage risk and protect profits. This could involve rolling out positions to a further expiration date, closing one side of the trade early, or adjusting strike prices in response to market movements. The decision-making process for adjustments is informed by real-time market data, with a keen eye on the trade's Greeks, especially delta and gamma, to gauge risk exposure.

Following the closure of the trade, a meticulous post-execution review is conducted. This analysis contrasts the initial strategy with the actual trade outcomes, scrutinizing every decision made and its impact on the trade's profitability. This review is not only about measuring success in financial terms but also about evaluating the decision-making process, the effectiveness of adjustments, and the trader's ability to remain disciplined under pressure.

Case Study: A Real-World Example

Consider a trade on the S&P 500 Index (SPX), where a trader establishes an iron condor in anticipation of a stable market. The chosen strike prices for the call and put spreads are strategically selected based on current volatility and market outlook, with an expiration 45 days away. Despite an unexpected spike in volatility two weeks into the trade, timely adjustments and a disciplined approach to risk management enable the trader to navigate the challenges effectively, resulting in a profitable outcome.

Trade execution within the iron condor strategy embodies the convergence of art and science—art in the adaptive and intuitive aspects of decision-making, and science in the analytical and strategic foundation upon which those decisions are made.

Mastery of trade execution is not achieved overnight but through consistent practice, reflection, and a relentless pursuit of knowledge. This detailed breakdown serves as a blueprint for traders aspiring to elevate their execution proficiency, turning strategic vision into operational success.

Initial Setup and Strategy

The foundational step in setting up an iron condor is laying out a strategic blueprint, which hinges on a thorough market analysis. This analysis encompasses a deep dive into the underlying asset's historical performance, volatility patterns, and market sentiments. The trader must also consider macroeconomic factors and specific events that could influence market dynamics during the lifespan of the iron condor.

The iron condor thrives in a market environment characterized by low to moderate volatility. Identifying such an environment requires a keen understanding of volatility indices such as the VIX (Volatility Index) for the broader market and the HV (Historical Volatility) and IV (Implied Volatility) for the specific underlying asset. The ideal scenario is when the IV is higher than HV, indicating that the market expects more movement than what has historically occurred, which typically results in higher premiums for the options sold.

The choice of the underlying asset is paramount. It should not only exhibit the liquidity necessary for smooth entry and exit but also display a propensity for range-bound behavior, aligning with the iron condor's requirement for the underlying asset to stay within a certain price range. Indexes, due to their aggregate nature, often present a viable option, reducing the risk of significant price swings caused by the news or events affecting individual companies.

The strategic selection of strike prices for the call and put options is a critical step that balances risk and reward. The strikes chosen for the sold options are typically out of the money, far enough to ensure a high probability of expiring worthless, yet close enough to collect a reasonable premium. The protective options bought are further out of the money, serving as insurance against significant market moves. The expiration date is typically set between 30 to 60 days in the future, optimizing the theta decay while providing a cushion against market volatility.

Entry into an iron condor is as much about timing as it is about preparation. Traders often look for a lull in market volatility or a stable period following a significant event when premiums remain inflated yet the likelihood of large swings decreases. The entry strategy involves simultaneously opening both the call and put spreads. This can be executed as separate transactions for each spread or, for more experienced traders, as a single four-leg trade to potentially improve the execution rate and reduce commission costs.

Before entering the trade, setting predetermined risk management parameters is crucial. This includes deciding on maximum loss thresholds and identifying conditions under which the trade will be adjusted or exited. These parameters are informed by the trader's risk tolerance and capital allocation strategy.

Case Study: Strategic Entry

Imagine a scenario where a trader is eyeing the S&P 500 ETF (SPY) for an iron condor setup. After a period of heightened volatility, the VIX begins to stabilize, signaling an opportunity.

The trader selects strike prices for the call and put spreads that are aligned with the SPY's historical price range and opts for an expiration 45 days out. The trade is entered during a quiet market morning to avoid slippage, with each leg filled at favorable premiums. The trader sets a maximum acceptable loss at 20% of the premium received and plans for adjustments if the delta of any sold option exceeds 30, indicating a move closer to being in the money.

The initial setup and strategy of an iron condor are critical to its success. This meticulous preparation phase sets the stage for the nuanced management and adjustment strategies that follow. With a solid foundation, traders can confidently navigate the complexities of the iron condor, optimizing their potential for profit while managing risk in this sophisticated strategy.

Mid-trade Adjustments

The decision to adjust an iron condor mid-trade hinges on several key indicators. Market movement that threatens the boundaries of our iron condor, significant changes in volatility, and approaching economic events can all signal the need for action. The adept trader monitors these indicators closely, prepared to pivot as conditions evolve.

Strategies for Adjustment: A Toolkit

- Rolling Out or Up/Down: One common strategy involves "rolling" the threatened side of the iron condor (either calls or puts) to higher or lower strike prices, respectively, or extending the expiration to buy time for the market to stabilize. This maneuver requires a delicate balance, trading off immediate risk for potential future exposure.

- Adding Spreads: Another tactic is to add additional call or put spreads to the non-threatened side of the iron condor, increasing the premium to offset potential losses. This approach, while increasing potential returns, also raises the maximum risk.

- Closing Out Part of the Position: In some cases, the most prudent action is to close out the most threatened part of the position, either the call or put spread, to lock in partial profits or cut losses. This decision often hinges on a reassessment of the market's direction and volatility.

Case Study: Dynamic Adjustment in Action

Consider a trader who has established an iron condor on the NASDAQ 100 index, aiming for a serene passage through the market's fluctuations. Suddenly, a tech sector rally pushes the index upwards, threatening the call spread of the iron condor. The trader, vigilant and responsive, decides to roll up the call spread to higher strikes, simultaneously extending the expiration by one month. This adjustment requires an additional outlay of capital but liberates the position from immediate danger, offering the market more room to oscillate without breaching the iron condor's boundaries.

Mid-trade adjustments are not just a test of strategy but of psychology. The emotional discipline to execute adjustments without succumbing to panic or greed is paramount. Traders must cultivate a mindset of detachment, viewing the iron condor as a dynamic puzzle to be solved rather than a win-or-lose proposition.

The efficacy of mid-trade adjustments cannot be judged in the heat of the moment but through post-trade reflection. Key metrics include the adjustment's impact on the overall risk/reward profile, the costs incurred through additional commissions and spreads, and the eventual outcome of the trade. Continuous learning from each adjustment— both successful and otherwise—is essential for refining one's approach to iron condor trading.

Mid-trade adjustments are a critical component of the iron condor strategy, demanding a fusion of market insight, strategic finesse, and emotional control. By understanding the conditions that necessitate adjustments and mastering the techniques to execute them effectively, traders can enhance their capacity to navigate the complexities of the market, safeguarding their positions against unforeseen shifts and capitalizing on the opportunities these movements present. This journey through the mid-trade adjustment phase underscores the iterative process of learning, adapting, and evolving that defines the essence of successful trading.

The climax of the iron condor strategy unfolds as the trader approaches the critical juncture of closing the position. This pivotal moment encapsulates the culmination of careful planning, precise execution, and strategic adjustments, leading to the final act of realizing or mitigating losses. The closure of an iron condor position is not merely a transactional occurrence but a strategic decision that reflects the trader's adaptability, foresight, and risk management acumen.

Strategic Considerations for Closing the Position

Closing an iron condor position demands a nuanced

understanding of market conditions, the specific goals of the trade, and the current performance of the position. Several factors influence the decision to close:

- Achieving Target Profit: If the position has reached a predefined profit target before expiration, closing early to lock in gains might be wise. This decision balances the potential for additional profit against the risk of market reversal.

- Mitigating Losses: Conversely, if the market moves unfavorably, closing the position before maximum loss thresholds are breached can be a prudent damage control strategy. This requires a keen sense of market direction and volatility.

- Expiration Approaches: As expiration nears, the gamma risk —the sensitivity of an option's delta to market movements —intensifies. Traders may choose to close positions to avoid the unpredictability of last-minute price swings or the consequences of options being exercised.

Techniques for Closing the Position

- Unwinding the Spread: The most straightforward method of closing an iron condor is to simultaneously buy back the sold options and sell the bought options, effectively unwinding the position. This action requires careful timing to optimize the exit price.

- Legging Out: In some cases, traders may close each leg of the iron condor separately, seeking to maximize profit or minimize loss on each component. This approach carries additional risk due to market movement during the interval between closing each leg.

- Exercising Options: Rarely, it may be advantageous to exercise one or more options in the condor if the underlying asset's price makes this favorable. This is typically reserved for scenarios where exercising yields a better outcome than selling the option.

Case Study: Timely Exit from Turbulence

Imagine a scenario where a trader has an iron condor position on the S&P 500 ETF. A sudden geopolitical event triggers a market downturn, significantly threatening the put spread side of the condor. Recognizing the potential for further decline, the trader decides to close the position, unwinding the spreads to recoup a portion of the initial premium and avoid a total loss. This decisive action underscores the importance of being attuned to global events and their market impacts.

The decision to close an iron condor position also navigates complex psychological terrain. Traders must confront the emotional pull of greed and fear—greed that tempts holding a position too long in hopes of greater profit, and fear that may provoke premature closure. Mastery over these impulses, through disciplined risk management and objective decision-making, is crucial for long-term success.

Post-closure analysis is invaluable, offering insights into the trade's execution, the effectiveness of adjustments, and the accuracy of market predictions. This reflective practice enables traders to distill lessons from each trade, refining their strategy, enhancing their market intuition, and bolstering their psychological resilience.

The Art and Science of Concluding Iron Condor Trades

In the aftermath of an iron condor position, the astute trader embarks on a journey of introspection and analysis. This reflective phase is not merely a review; it is an essential pillar of strategy development and personal growth in the art of options trading. The lessons gleaned from each closing provide the raw material for honing one's approach to the markets, emphasizing the importance of continuous learning and adaptation.

Key Takeaways from Closing Iron Condor Positions

- Objective Evaluation: Independent of the trade's outcome, an objective evaluation of the decision-making process, from entry to exit, is crucial. This analysis should dissect the trade's rationale, the timing of adjustments, and the factors influencing the decision to close.

- Market Behavior Insights: Each trade offers a window into the dynamics of market behavior, particularly in response to external stimuli such as economic reports, geopolitical events, or shifts in market sentiment. Understanding these reactions enhances future strategy alignment with market conditions.

- Risk Management Reinforcement: The core of successful iron condor trading lies in effective risk management. Reviewing closed positions reinforces the importance of predefined risk parameters and the discipline required to adhere to them, even under pressure.

- Psychological Fortitude: Trading, particularly strategies involving complex instruments like iron condors, tests one's emotional and psychological mettle. Lessons in emotional discipline, patience, and the ability to detach from the monetary aspects of trading are invaluable takeaways.

Detailed Case Analysis: A Reflective Practice

Consider a detailed case study where a trader initiated an iron condor on a major index, expecting low volatility, but was met with unexpected market turbulence. The analysis would delve into the initial assumptions, the impact of unforeseen volatility, and the decision-making process leading to the trade's closure. This case study would examine the adjustments made (or not made) and explore alternative strategies that could have mitigated the outcome. The reflective practice encourages a deeper understanding of the trade's context, the efficacy of the chosen strategy under those circumstances, and the trader's psychological responses throughout the trade lifecycle.

Incorporating Lessons into Future Strategies

- Adaptability: Flexibility in strategy, particularly in response to market indicators and volatility, is a critical lesson. Future trades benefit from an enhanced ability to pivot as market conditions dictate.

- Preparation for Contingencies: Understanding that not all variables can be controlled or predicted, but preparing for a range of outcomes, strengthens future trade planning and execution.

- Emphasizing Process Over Outcome: Focusing on the integrity of the trading process, rather than the financial outcome of individual trades, promotes long-term consistency and success.

The closure of an iron condor position and the subsequent analysis is not merely an end but a stepping stone to greater mastery of options trading. The lessons learned and the key takeaways distilled from each trade form the foundation of a trader's evolution. This reflective process, rooted in objectivity, rigor, and a commitment to continuous improvement, is indispensable for navigating the complexities of the market with confidence and strategic acuity. Through this lens, each trade, regardless of its immediate outcome, contributes to the trader's development and the refinement of their trading philosophy, underscoring the journey of growth that lies successful trading.

Strategic Insights

Fostering a nuanced understanding of the iron condor strategy extends beyond the mechanics of trade execution to encompass strategic insights that define the contours of success. This segment illuminates the deeper strategic considerations that should guide the application of iron condors within the broader context of an investor's portfolio and market movements. The insights gathered here are distilled from the crucible of market realities, embodying wisdom that can only be earned through experience.

Strategic Framework for Iron Condor Trading

- Alignment with Market Outlook: The decision to deploy an iron condor should not occur in isolation but as part of a strategic response to one's analysis of market conditions. Iron condors thrive in environments characterized by low to moderate volatility. However, the savvy trader will recognize when to adjust the wings of the condor—widening or tightening —in response to subtle shifts in market sentiment or volatility forecasts.

- Portfolio Synergy: Iron condors should be viewed not just as standalone positions but as components of a diversified portfolio. Their role? To provide stability and generate income amidst the ebb and flow of market dynamics. Strategic insights emphasize the integration of iron condors with other positions to balance risk, leverage correlations, and achieve a desired portfolio exposure to market movements.

- Capital Allocation: Effective capital management is paramount. Strategic insights highlight the importance of allocating only a portion of one's capital to iron condors, preserving liquidity, and maintaining flexibility to adjust positions or capitalize on unforeseen opportunities. This prudent approach mitigates the risk of overexposure to a single strategy or market event.

- Adjustment Strategy: Anticipation and preparation for adjustment are strategic imperatives. Insightful traders develop a playbook of adjustment strategies tailored to various market scenarios, allowing them to respond proactively rather than reactively. This includes widening spreads, rolling positions, or employing defensive strategies to protect against losses.

Leveraging Insights for Decision Making

Each trade in the iron condor universe offers a compendium of lessons. Strategic insights urge traders to cultivate a habit of rigorous post-trade analysis, extracting actionable intelligence to refine decision-making processes. This discipline transforms raw market data and trade outcomes into a strategic asset.

- Scenario Planning: Developing a range of scenarios based on historical market behavior and current market analysis can guide the selection of strike prices, durations, and adjustments. This forward-looking strategy empowers traders to navigate uncertainty with informed agility.

- Psychological Resilience: The strategic insight extends to the trader's mindset, advocating for resilience, discipline, and the cultivation of an even-keeled approach to the vicissitudes of trading. Recognizing the psychological pitfalls inherent in trading—such as overconfidence in winning streaks or despondency in losses—is crucial for maintaining strategic clarity.

Strategic Mastery

The journey through iron condor trading is one of continuous learning and strategic refinement. The insights presented here are not merely tactical maneuvers but pillars of a broader strategic vision. They underscore the importance of adaptability, portfolio harmony, disciplined capital management, and the psychological fortitude necessary to navigate the markets effectively.

As traders assimilate these strategic insights into their approach, they transcend the mechanical aspects of the iron condor strategy, embracing a holistic view that integrates market analysis, risk management, and personal discipline. This strategic alchemy is the hallmark of mastery in options trading, enabling traders to not only survive but thrive in the ever-changing tapestry of the financial markets.

Risk Management Best Practices

- Clearly Defined Risk Parameters: Before entering any trade, the iron condor trader must establish clear risk parameters. This involves deciding the maximum percentage of the portfolio that can be risked on a single trade and the total exposure the portfolio should have to iron condor positions. By setting these parameters, traders preemptively limit potential losses, ensuring they align with their risk tolerance and trading objectives.

- Use of Stop-Loss Orders: While the iron condor is inherently a defined risk strategy, employing stop-loss orders on individual legs of the condor can further protect against unforeseen market moves. This practice involves setting predetermined levels at which positions will be automatically closed to prevent further losses, hence adding an extra layer of risk mitigation.

- Regular Portfolio Review: The dynamic nature of financial markets necessitates regular reviews of the trading portfolio. This entails assessing the performance of individual iron condor positions and the portfolio's overall exposure to market volatility. Adjustments should be made in response to changing market conditions, ensuring the portfolio remains aligned with the trader's risk appetite and investment goals.

Strategic Diversification within Iron Condor Trading

Diversification is a cornerstone of risk management, and within the context of iron condor trading, it takes on a multifaceted approach:

- Temporal Diversification: Spreading trades across different expiration dates can help mitigate the risk associated with specific market events or periods of heightened volatility. This approach smoothens the portfolio's performance curve over time, reducing the impact of any single trade outcome.

- Underlying Asset Diversification: Employing iron condors on a variety of underlying assets—ranging from indices to individual stocks—reduces the trader's exposure to the idiosyncratic risk of any single asset. It's crucial, however, to ensure that these assets are not highly correlated, as this could inadvertently increase portfolio risk.

CHAPTER 8:
QUANTITATIVE
TECHNIQUES
AND TOOLS

I n options trading, the application of quantitative techniques and tools stands as a cornerstone of modern trading methodologies. This segment delves into the world of quantitative analysis, focusing on its pivotal role in optimizing trading strategies, enhancing decision-making processes, and managing risk with precision. It elucidates the essential quantitative tools that traders must master to thrive in the dynamic environment of financial markets.

The Essence of Quantitative Analysis in Options Trading

- Foundation of Quantitative Techniques: quantitative analysis involves the use of mathematical and statistical models to predict market movements and evaluate trading strategies. In the context of iron condors, quantitative techniques enable traders to assess the probability of profit, calculate potential risk and return, and identify optimal entry and exit points.

- Role of Quantitative Tools: Various software and platforms offer advanced quantitative tools designed to analyze market data, execute trades, and monitor positions in real time. These tools are indispensable for traders aiming to implement iron condor strategies effectively, allowing for the meticulous management of multiple positions across different underlying assets.

Key Quantitative Techniques and Tools

- Option Pricing Models: The Black-Scholes model and binomial models are pivotal in calculating the theoretical value of options. Understanding these models empowers traders to price iron condors accurately, making informed decisions based on the intrinsic and time value of options contracts.

- Monte Carlo Simulations: This technique allows traders to model the probability distribution of potential outcomes for an iron condor strategy under various market scenarios. By simulating thousands of random price paths, traders can gauge the risk and potential profitability of their positions.

- Risk Assessment Tools: Quantitative tools such as Delta, Gamma, Theta, and Vega—collectively known as "the Greeks"— are critical in assessing the risk exposure of iron condor positions. These metrics help traders understand how their positions are likely to react to changes in the market, such as shifts in the underlying price, time decay, and volatility.

- Value at Risk (VaR) and Stress Testing: VaR provides a quantitative measure of the maximum expected loss over a specified time period, under normal market conditions.

Stress testing complements VaR by simulating extreme market conditions to evaluate how iron condor positions might perform during market turmoil.

Integrating Quantitative Tools into Trading Strategies

- Software and Technology: Traders must familiarize themselves with the latest software and technology that offer robust quantitative analysis capabilities. Platforms that provide real-time analytics, automated trading options, and comprehensive risk management features are essential for executing iron condor strategies efficiently.

- Data-Driven Decision Making: The essence of quantitative trading lies in making decisions grounded in data analysis rather than intuition. By leveraging quantitative tools, traders can systematically evaluate the viability of their iron condor setups, adjust positions in response to market changes, and enhance their overall trading performance.

- Continuous Learning and Adaptation: The field of quantitative analysis is ever-evolving, with new models, algorithms, and technologies emerging regularly. Traders must commit to ongoing education to stay abreast of the latest developments and incorporate them into their trading arsenal.

The Essence of Option Pricing Models

In Options trading lies a critical question: How do we determine the fair value of an option? This query is not merely academic but pulsates through the daily decisions of traders worldwide. The answer lies within the realms of option pricing models – sophisticated mathematical frameworks designed to calculate the theoretical value of options based on various factors including the underlying asset's price, volatility, time until expiration, and the risk-free rate of return.

The Black-Scholes model, a name that resonates with reverence in the options trading community, was a groundbreaking development in financial theory. Introduced in 1973 by Fischer Black, Myron Scholes, and albeit indirectly, Robert Merton, this model provided the first closed-form solution for pricing European-style options. Its beauty lies in its simplicity and the elegance with which it distilled the complex nature of market forces into a comprehensible formula.

The Black-Scholes equation considers the current stock price, the option's strike price, the time to expiration, the risk-free interest rate, and the stock's volatility to compute the option's price. Yet, for all its brilliance, the model assumes a world of log-normal asset price movements, constant volatility, and a lack of dividends, which can diverge from the messy reality of financial markets.

Binomial Option Pricing: A Step Towards Flexibility

The binomial option pricing model introduces a more versatile approach to option valuation. Developed by Cox, Ross, and Rubinstein in 1979, this model employs a lattice-based structure that allows for multiple possible price paths for the underlying asset. Each node in the lattice represents a possible price at a future date, and the option value is determined by back-calculating from the option's expiration to the present.

This model's adaptability lies in its capacity to adjust for dividends and multiple time steps, enabling a more nuanced view of an option's time value and providing valuable insights into American-style options, which can be exercised before expiration.

Beyond Black-Scholes and Binomial: The Advent of Computational Finance

As computational power surged, so did the complexity and accuracy of option pricing models. Monte Carlo simulations, named after the famous casino for their reliance on randomness, offer a powerful tool for pricing options with multiple sources of uncertainty or with path-dependent features. By simulating thousands or even millions of potential price paths for the underlying asset, Monte Carlo methods can approximate the pricing of highly complex derivatives that are beyond the reach of closed-form solutions.

The Significance of The Greeks in Option Pricing

Understanding option pricing models requires familiarity with "The Greeks" - delta, gamma, theta, and vega. These risk measures describe how the price of an option changes in response to changes in underlying factors like the price of the stock, time, and volatility. Traders leverage The Greeks to hedge their portfolios, manage risk, and make informed decisions on the fly.

Option pricing models are not just mathematical constructs but are the very fabric that connects theory with practice in options trading. They equip traders with the insights needed to navigate the markets, manage risk, and capitalize on opportunities. As we continue to evolve our understanding and computational methods, these models will undoubtedly be refined, but their foundational importance to options trading will remain unchanged.

In the next sections, we will explore the practical application of these models in real-world trading scenarios, shedding light on their utility and limitations. Through this exploration, traders will be empowered with the knowledge to harness the full potential of option pricing models, crafting strategies that resonate with the rhythms of the market.

The Black-Scholes Model: Decoding the Genius

the Black-Scholes model is governed by a partial differential equation that captures the dynamics of options pricing. The elegance of the formula lies in its simplicity and the profound insight it offers into the valuation of European options—options that can only be exercised at expiration. The equation integrates several variables: the current price of the stock (S), the strike price of the option (K), the time to expiration (T), the risk-free rate (r), and the volatility of the stock's returns (σ).

One of the model's hallmark contributions is its derivation of an explicit formula for the price of a call option, with a parallel methodology applicable for put options through put-call parity. This analytical solution, a rarity in the complex domain of financial derivatives, demystifies the valuation process, equipping traders with a powerful tool to assess options in real-time.

The Black-Scholes model rests on a set of assumptions that create a pristine, though somewhat idealized, world. These include the log-normal distribution of stock prices, constant volatility and interest rates, and the absence of dividends. While these assumptions facilitate a clean, analytical solution, they also represent the model's most significant limitations. Real-world deviations from these assumptions—such as dynamic volatility and the impact of dividends on stock prices—necessitate refinements and extensions to the original model.

The introduction of the Black-Scholes model revolutionized options trading, providing a systematic method to price options that did not rely solely on intuition and experience. The model's insights into the "Greeks"—Delta (Δ), Gamma (Γ), Theta (Θ), Vega (ν), and Rho (ρ)—have become indispensable tools for traders. These risk metrics allow traders to construct hedged portfolios, design arbitrage strategies, and manage risk with a degree of sophistication and accuracy that was previously unattainable.

In response to the limitations of the Black-Scholes model, the finance community has developed extensions and alternatives that accommodate more complex market conditions. The introduction of models that account for stochastic volatility and jump diffusion processes reflects the ongoing evolution of options pricing theory. These advancements strive to bridge the gap between the theoretical world of Black-Scholes and the multifaceted reality of financial markets.

Despite its assumptions and the emergence of more sophisticated models, the Black-Scholes formula remains a testament to the power of mathematical finance. Its impact extends beyond options pricing, influencing the broader field of financial engineering and risk management. As traders and academics continue to build on its foundation, the Black-Scholes model stands as a pivotal milestone in the journey to understand and navigate the complexities of the financial markets.

In the subsequent sections, we will delve into the practical applications and limitations of the Black-Scholes model in contemporary trading, exploring how traders can leverage its strengths while mitigating its weaknesses. Through this exploration, we aim to equip readers with a nuanced understanding of options pricing and the strategic application of the Black-Scholes model in optimizing their trading decisions.

Binomial Models: Unfolding Layers of Option Pricing

At its heart, the Binomial model provides a methodical way to value options by creating a price tree that branches out over successive time intervals until the option's expiration. Each node on this tree represents a possible future price of the underlying asset, with the branches denoting the rise or fall in price over each interval. This bifurcation process echoes the binary outcomes inherent in options—exercise or expiry, encapsulating the probabilistic nature of financial markets.

The construction of a Binomial lattice starts with defining the up and down factors, which dictate the percentage change in the underlying asset's price for each upward or downward move. These factors hinge on the volatility of the asset and the length of the time steps. Central to this model is the concept of risk-neutral valuation, which assumes that investors are indifferent to risk. Under this framework, the expected return on the asset is equal to the risk-free rate, allowing for the simplification of the option pricing process.

One of the Binomial model's most lauded attributes is its flexibility. The model can accommodate options that offer payouts at multiple times (American options), as well as those with complex features such as callability and putability. This adaptability makes the Binomial model particularly suitable for pricing American options, where the option to exercise early introduces additional layers of complexity.

In practical terms, the Binomial model enables traders to dissect the path-dependent nature of options, illuminating how prices evolve and diverge with each passing interval. By simulating different scenarios, traders can gauge the sensitivity of an option's price to various factors—time to expiration, underlying volatility, and changes in interest rates. This insight is invaluable for constructing hedged portfolios that can withstand the vicissitudes of market dynamics.

Despite its advantages, the Binomial model is not without its limitations. The accuracy of the model relies heavily on the chosen time step size—the smaller the steps, the more precise the model, but at the cost of increased computational complexity. Furthermore, the assumption of a constant risk-free rate and volatility over the life of the option is a simplification that may not hold in the tumultuous real-world markets.

As we peel away the layers of the Binomial options pricing model, its enduring relevance in the finance world becomes evident. Its conceptual simplicity, coupled with the depth of analysis it offers, makes it a powerful tool for understanding and navigating the complexities of option pricing. While it serves as a complement rather than a competitor to the Black-Scholes model, the Binomial model's discrete approach offers a different perspective on the intrinsic value of options—a perspective that enriches the trader's strategic arsenal.

In the grand tapestry of financial models, the Binomial model stands out for its practical insights and its capacity to model the nuanced realities of option trading. As we venture further into options strategies, the foundational understanding gleaned from the Binomial model will serve as a guiding light, illuminating the path to informed and strategic decision-making in the options trading arena.

Monte Carlo Simulations: Harnessing Randomness for Precision

Beneath the veneer of market predictability, lies a realm of stochasticity and chaos. This is the domain where Monte Carlo simulations thrive, offering a prism through which the multifaceted uncertainties of financial markets can be both examined and understood. Far from being a gamble, these simulations serve as a sophisticated tool in the arsenal of an options trader, especially when navigating the complexities of iron condor strategies. This segment delves into Monte Carlo simulations, unraveling their principles, applications, and intrinsic value in options pricing and risk assessment.

Monte Carlo simulations derive their name from the famed casino in Monaco, symbolizing the inherent randomness and uncertainty they aim to model. the Monte Carlo method employs randomness to solve problems that might be deterministic in principle. This technique involves generating a large number of random samples to model phenomena, thereby allowing for the approximation of complex mathematical or physical systems' behaviors.

In the context of options trading, Monte Carlo simulations offer a dynamic framework for pricing options under a myriad of market conditions. The method starts by simulating thousands, if not millions, of potential paths for the underlying asset's price over the option's life. Each path represents a possible future, traced by randomly generating price movements based on the statistical properties of historical data, such as mean returns and volatility.

These simulated paths provide a distribution of possible outcomes, from which the value of an option can be inferred. By calculating the payoff for each path and then averaging these payoffs, discounted back to present value at the risk-free rate, traders can obtain an estimate of the option's fair value.

For traders wielding iron condors—a strategy that thrives on market stability and slight fluctuations—Monte Carlo simulations offer a prophetic glimpse into the strategy's viability under varying market conditions. By simulating a range of price movements within the bounds of an iron condor setup, traders can assess the probability of the underlying asset breaching the strategy's break-even points. This analysis is pivotal in adjusting the strikes and widths of the condor legs to optimize the risk-reward ratio.

Monte Carlo simulations extend their utility beyond mere options pricing into risk assessment and management. By simulating diverse market scenarios, traders can stress-test their portfolios against extreme market movements, identifying potential vulnerabilities. This foresight enables the formulation of contingency plans, be it through strategic adjustments to the positions or by employing protective measures like stop-losses.

Despite their robustness, Monte Carlo simulations are not without limitations. The accuracy of the simulation is contingent upon the model's assumptions about market behavior, which may not always capture future uncertainties. Hence, while these simulations are a powerful tool for envisioning potential market scenarios, they should be employed as part of a broader strategic framework that considers both quantitative analysis and qualitative market insights.

Monte Carlo simulations represent a confluence of randomness and precision, offering traders a nuanced lens through which to view the probabilistic nature of financial markets. In the strategic deployment of iron condors, these simulations serve not just as a tool for valuation, but as a guide for navigating the tumultuous seas of options trading. They remind us that in financial markets, embracing uncertainty with a calculated approach can transform randomness into a strategic ally. As we chart our course through the complexities of options strategies, the insights gleaned from Monte Carlo simulations stand as beacons, guiding us towards informed decision-making and strategic acumen in our trading endeavors.

Risk Assessment Tools: Navigating the Uncertainties of Options Trading

risk management lies the fundamental question: "What is at stake?" This query extends beyond mere monetary valuation, probing into the probabilities of various market outcomes and their impacts on an options portfolio. Risk assessment tools are engineered to provide clarity on this front, leveraging mathematical models, statistical analysis, and market data to forecast potential losses and identify strategies' vulnerabilities.

1. Value at Risk (VaR): A cornerstone in the edifice of risk management, Value at Risk quantifies the maximum loss expected over a set period at a specific confidence level. For iron condor traders, VaR offers a lens to glimpse potential losses under normal market conditions, assisting in the calibration of strategy thresholds to maintain losses within acceptable bounds.

2. Delta, Gamma, Theta, Vega - The Greeks: The Greeks serve as the Rosetta Stone for options traders, translating the sensitivity of an option's price to various factors — market movements (Delta), time decay (Theta), volatility (Vega), and acceleration of Delta (Gamma). In deploying iron condors, understanding these metrics is paramount in optimizing the strategy to withstand market gyrations and time's erosion.

3. Beta Weighting: A technique used for portfolio risk assessment, beta weighting contextualizes the portfolio's volatility against a benchmark index. This tool enables traders to gauge how external market movements are likely to influence their iron condor positions, facilitating adjustments to hedge against systemic market risks.

4. Stress Testing and Scenario Analysis: By simulating extreme market conditions (stress testing) and varying market scenarios (scenario analysis), traders can assess the resilience of their iron condor strategies against unforeseen market upheavals. These tools are instrumental in identifying potential break points in a strategy, allowing for preemptive adjustments.

5. Monte Carlo Simulations: As previously discussed, Monte Carlo simulations offer predictive insights into the probabilistic outcomes of an iron condor strategy under a plethora of market conditions, aiding in both strategy formulation and risk assessment.

The integration of risk assessment tools into iron condor trading is not merely a best practice but a necessity for navigating the market's uncertainties. These tools provide a multidimensional view of risk, from the macroscopic market trends to the microscopic adjustments in option pricing due to time or volatility changes. By employing a combination of these tools, traders can sculpt iron condor strategies that are not only resilient but also adaptable to the market's ebbs and flows.

The strategic application of risk assessment tools in iron condor trading hinges on balance. It involves calibrating the position to optimize the risk-reward ratio while maintaining the flexibility to adjust as market conditions evolve. This balancing act requires a vigilant eye on the metrics provided by risk assessment tools and a readiness to pivot strategy in response to their forecasts.

Risk assessment tools are the navigator's instruments in the vast ocean of options trading, guiding traders through the fog of market volatility and the currents of time decay. For the iron condor strategist, these tools are indispensable, offering the insights needed to chart a course through the complex interplay of risk and reward. As we delve further into the mechanics of iron condor trading, the lessons learned from these tools will form the bedrock of our strategies, steering us towards informed decisions and prudent risk management in our trading voyage.

Delta, Gamma, Theta, Vega: Demystifying the Greeks in Options Trading

Delta, the first of the Greeks, measures an option's sensitivity to changes in the price of the underlying asset. It is represented as a numerical value between -1 and 1 for puts and 0 and 1 for calls. In iron condors, Delta serves as a critical gauge of the position's directional bias. A Delta near 0 indicates a neutral stance, aligning perfectly with the iron condor's strategy of capitalizing on a range-bound market. However, the vigilant trader monitors Delta closely, ready to adjust the wings of the condor should the market begin to show a clear direction, ensuring the strategy remains grounded in neutrality.

While Delta tells us about the direction of the wind, Gamma reveals the speed of the changing wind. It measures the rate of change in Delta for a one-point move in the underlying asset. For the iron condor trader, Gamma's importance cannot be overstated. A high Gamma indicates a volatile market environment where Delta, and thus the price sensitivity of options, changes rapidly. In such scenarios, the trader's adeptness in managing Gamma—by adjusting the position to maintain a low Gamma—ensures the stability of the iron condor, protecting it against sudden market gusts.

Theta, often termed as the silent assassin of options, measures the rate at which an option's value decreases over time, all else being equal. For iron condors, Theta represents a double-edged sword. On one side, the strategy profits from the relentless march of time, as the premium paid for the options decays towards expiry. On the other, a poorly timed or structured iron condor can suffer from adverse Theta, eroding potential profits. Thus, the astute trader employs Theta to their advantage, structuring the condor to maximize time decay while guarding against premature erosion.

Vega measures the sensitivity of an option's price to changes in the volatility of the underlying asset. It is the breath of the market, inhaling and exhaling as sentiment and conditions shift. In the strategic design of iron condors, Vega plays a pivotal role. A high Vega indicates a volatile market, with options prices more sensitive to changes in implied volatility. Conversely, a low Vega suggests a calm market. The iron condor strategist aims to construct a position that benefits from a decrease in volatility (negative Vega), as this typically corresponds with the stabilization of prices within the condor's favorable range.

Mastering the Greeks in iron condor trading is akin to conducting a symphony; each Greek must be harmonized with the others to create a cohesive strategy. The trader balances Delta to maintain neutrality, manages Gamma to mitigate rapid changes, leverages Theta for time decay, and navigates Vega to benefit from volatility adjustments. It is through this dance with the Greeks that iron condor traders can achieve a position of strength, poised to capitalize on the market's nuances.

Understanding Delta, Gamma, Theta, and Vega is paramount for any trader wishing to navigate the complex seas of options trading successfully. These Greeks provide the compass by which iron condor strategies can be aligned with market conditions, offering a roadmap to profitability. As we continue our journey through the exploration of iron condor trading, the insights gleaned from the Greeks will serve as our guiding light, ensuring our strategies are both robust and resilient in the face of market vicissitudes.

Value at Risk (VaR): The Sentinel of Risk Management in Options Trading

Value at Risk (VaR) is a statistical technique used to measure and quantify the level of financial risk within a firm, portfolio, or position over a specific time frame. This metric offers traders and risk managers a clear and concise way to assess potential losses in the face of market volatility. VaR is typically expressed as a maximum potential loss (in currency terms) and a confidence level over a set period. For example, a one-day 95% VaR of $1 million suggests that there is a 95% chance that the portfolio's loss will not exceed $1 million in a single day.

For traders employing the iron condor strategy, understanding and applying VaR is indispensable. The iron condor, a neutral strategy designed to profit from low volatility in the underlying asset, requires meticulous risk management to navigate through periods of unexpected market turbulence. VaR provides a framework for traders to assess the potential risks associated with their iron condor positions, considering the combined exposure of the put and call spreads that constitute the strategy.

The calculation of VaR for iron condor positions involves considering the net exposure of the strategy to price movements in the underlying asset, as well as to changes in volatility. There are several methods to calculate VaR, including:

- Historical Simulation: This approach uses historical market data to simulate potential future losses. For an iron condor trader, historical simulation would involve analyzing how the strategy would have performed during past market conditions, providing insights into potential future risks.

- Variance-Covariance Method: This method assumes that returns on assets are normally distributed and uses the standard deviation of historical returns as a measure of risk. For an iron condor, the variance-covariance method would assess the sensitivity of the position to movements in the underlying asset and changes in volatility.

- Monte Carlo Simulation: This technique uses computer algorithms to simulate a wide range of possible market conditions and calculate the potential losses in each scenario. For iron condors, Monte Carlo simulations can model the impact of shifts in the underlying asset's price and volatility on the strategy's performance.

The integration of VaR into the risk management process enables iron condor traders to quantify their potential exposure to adverse market movements. By understanding the worst-case scenarios at a given confidence level, traders can make informed decisions about position sizing, entry and exit points, and when to adjust or close positions to mitigate risk. Furthermore, VaR can be instrumental in portfolio diversification, helping traders to balance their iron condor positions with other strategies to optimize the risk-return profile.

Value at Risk (VaR) emerges as a pivotal tool in the arsenal of iron condor traders, offering a quantified perspective on potential losses. In the ballet of options trading, where each movement can have significant financial implications, VaR serves as a beacon, guiding traders through the uncertain seas of market volatility. As we advance further into the complexities of options trading strategies, the principles and applications of VaR will remain integral to mastering risk and safeguarding profits in the ever-changing financial markets.

Stress Testing and Scenario Analysis: Navigating Through Financial Storms in Iron Condor Trading

Stress testing involves simulating extreme market conditions ("stress scenarios") to evaluate the potential impact on an investment portfolio's value, particularly focusing on outlier events that, while rare, can induce significant financial strain. For traders wielding the iron condor strategy, stress testing is a lens through which the vulnerabilities of their positions are magnified, revealing the potential for loss in tumultuous markets.

The essence of stress testing lies in its ability to answer "what-if" questions:

- What if the market plunges or soars dramatically?

- What if volatility spikes to unprecedented levels?

- What if a geopolitical event causes a market panic?

Answering these questions, traders can assess their strategy's resilience and adjust their positions to mitigate potential losses.

While stress testing is focused on specific stress factors, scenario analysis takes a broader view, considering multiple factors to create detailed narratives of potential future market conditions. This method involves constructing hypothetical scenarios based on a combination of historical events and forward-looking assumptions. For the iron condor trader, scenario analysis offers a narrative-driven approach to envisioning possible futures where the interplay of price movement, volatility, and time decay could affect their positions.

Scenario analysis in iron condor trading might involve scenarios such as:

- A sudden market correction similar to past financial crises.

- A period of low volatility persisting far longer than historical norms.

- A rapid shift in market sentiment due to technological breakthroughs or regulatory changes.

The integration of stress testing and scenario analysis into iron condor trading strategies equips traders with a deeper understanding of potential risks and rewards. This process not only highlights vulnerabilities but also identifies opportunities for strategy optimization. A systematic approach to incorporating these analyses might involve:

- Regularly conducting stress tests and updating scenarios to reflect current market conditions and forecasts.

- Using the insights gained to adjust the strike prices, widths of the spreads, and position sizes of iron condors to balance risk and reward effectively.

- Developing contingency plans for rapid strategy adjustments in response to unfolding market events predicted by scenario analysis.

Advancements in financial technology have empowered traders with sophisticated software tools for conducting stress testing and scenario analysis with greater precision and efficiency. These tools can simulate a wide array of market conditions and automatically calculate the potential impacts on iron condor positions, enabling traders to make data-driven decisions swiftly.

Stress testing and scenario analysis are not crystal balls granting omniscient foresight into the market's future but rather navigational aids in the vast and often turbulent sea of options trading. By systematically applying these methodologies, iron condor traders can fortify their positions against the unforeseen gales of the market, navigating through financial storms with informed confidence. This proactive stance on risk management does not eliminate risk but transforms it into a calculable factor that can be managed and mitigated, marking the difference between reactive survival and strategic thriving in the world of options trading.

Software and Technology for Iron Condor Trading: The Digital Wingman

The landscape of options trading has undergone a transformative evolution, transitioning from the manual, labor-intensive processes of the past to the streamlined, automated operations of today. Modern trading platforms are this transformation, equipped with features specifically designed to support the complex mechanics of iron condor strategies. These platforms offer:

- Real-time Market Data: Access to instantaneous market information, enabling traders to make informed decisions swiftly.

- Advanced Charting Tools: Visualization aids that allow traders to analyze market trends and forecast potential movements with greater accuracy.

- Automated Trade Execution: The ability to set precise entry and exit parameters for trades, ensuring that positions are executed at optimal times without the need for constant manual oversight.

Beyond the basic functionalities of trading platforms, specialized analytical software has become indispensable for iron condor traders seeking to decode the subtle signals of the options market. These tools leverage complex algorithms to sift through vast quantities of data, identifying patterns and trends that might elude the human eye. Key features include:

- Volatility Analysis: Tools that track historical and implied volatility, offering insights into potential market shifts that could impact the iron condor strategy.

- Risk Management Modules: Applications that simulate various market scenarios, as discussed in the previous section, allowing traders to assess the risk profile of their positions under different conditions.

- Optimization Algorithms: Software that recommends adjustments to strike prices and spread widths, aiming to maximize the profitability of iron condor positions while keeping risks in check.

The integration of automation and trading bots represents the frontier of technology in iron condor trading. These automated systems can monitor the market around the clock, executing trades, and making adjustments to positions based on predefined criteria. The benefits are twofold:

- Efficiency: Automation eliminates the need for constant manual monitoring, freeing traders to focus on strategy development and other high-value activities.

- Emotionless Trading: Bots operate based on algorithms, removing the emotional biases that can lead to suboptimal trading decisions.

However, while automation offers compelling advantages, it also necessitates a level of caution. Traders must ensure that they thoroughly understand the logic behind automated systems and continuously monitor their performance to guard against unforeseen market anomalies that could lead to losses.

Finally, technology plays a crucial role in the continuous education and community engagement of iron condor traders. Online forums, webinars, and virtual trading simulators provide platforms for traders to share strategies, learn from experienced mentors, and practice their skills in risk-free environments. This collective wisdom, facilitated by technology, enriches the trading community, fostering a culture of innovation and shared success.

The integration of software and technology into iron condor trading is not just a matter of convenience—it's a strategic imperative. As the trading environment becomes increasingly complex and dynamic, the digital wingman provides traders with the analytical prowess, executional precision, and risk management capabilities necessary to thrive. In embracing these digital tools, traders can navigate the iron condor landscape with greater confidence, leveraging technology to uncover opportunities and mitigate risks in their quest for financial success.

Best Platforms for Options Traders: The Ultimate Guide

In options trading, the choice of platform can be as critical to a trader's success as their strategy. While the previous section delved into the indispensable role of software and technology in trading iron condors, we now turn our focus to identifying the best platforms for options traders. These platforms stand out for their robust features, intuitive design, and comprehensive tools tailored to meet the nuanced needs of options trading, particularly strategies as as the iron condor.

The best platforms for options traders distinguish themselves through several key criteria:

- User Interface (UI) and Experience (UX): A clean, intuitive interface allows traders to navigate the platform efficiently, making swift trading decisions possible.

- Analytical Tools and Charting: Advanced charting capabilities and a suite of analytical tools are essential for dissecting market trends and crafting informed strategies.

- Speed and Reliability: In the fast-paced world of options trading, a platform's ability to execute trades quickly and without glitches can be the difference between profit and loss.

- Cost Structure: Competitive pricing, including commission rates and any hidden fees, significantly impacts the overall profitability of trading activities.

- Educational Resources and Support: The best platforms also provide traders with access to educational materials to refine their strategies and a support team ready to assist with any issues.

With these criteria in mind, the following platforms have been rigorously evaluated and identified as top choices for options traders:

- Thinkorswim by TD Ameritrade: Renowned for its comprehensive analytical tools and state-of-the-art charting capabilities, Thinkorswim caters to traders of all levels. Its platform offers a rich set of features, including real-time data streaming, customizable charts, and a wide array of technical indicators. The learning curve may be steep, but the platform's depth makes it worth the effort.

- Interactive Brokers (IB): A favorite among professional traders, Interactive Brokers provides access to a vast range of markets worldwide. Its pricing structure is particularly favorable for active traders, and its powerful Trader Workstation (TWS) platform comes packed with sophisticated analytical tools and risk management features.

- E*TRADE: With a more accessible interface, E*TRADE is a solid choice for both novice and experienced traders. Its options trading platform, Power E*TRADE, offers advanced charting tools, real-time quotes, and a plethora of educational resources to help traders navigate the options market.

- Robinhood: Known for its user-friendly mobile app and commission-free trading, Robinhood has made options trading accessible to a broader audience. While it lacks the advanced tools and features of its competitors, its simplicity makes it an attractive option for beginner traders.

- Tastyworks: Designed with options traders in mind, Tastyworks features an innovative interface that emphasizes options trading strategies, including iron condors. Its competitive pricing and focus on options trading community and education make it a standout platform for dedicated options traders.

While the platforms listed offer a range of compelling features, the choice ultimately hinges on the individual trader's needs, trading style, and strategy focus. For those specializing in iron condor trading, a platform that offers detailed analytical tools, robust risk management features, and competitive pricing will likely be the best fit.

The best platforms for options traders offer more than just the means to execute trades; they provide a strategic advantage in the form of advanced tools, insightful resources, and an intuitive trading environment. By carefully selecting a platform that aligns with their trading style and strategy, options traders can position themselves for greater success in the competitive world of options trading. Whether refining an iron condor strategy, analyzing market trends, or managing risk, the right platform is an invaluable ally on the journey to trading mastery.

Utilizing Software for Trade Management: A Deep Dive into Efficiency and Precision

Trade management software transcends the basic functionalities of placing and monitoring trades. It embodies a comprehensive ecosystem that facilitates strategic planning, execution, monitoring, and adjustment of trades with unparalleled precision. The essence of deploying such software lies in its capacity to provide traders with a granular view of their positions, real-time market data, and predictive analytics, all of which are crucial for informed decision-making.

- Strategic Execution: Advanced software platforms enable traders to automate their trading strategies, including the precise execution of iron condors. By setting predefined criteria for entry and exit points, traders can ensure the disciplined execution of their strategies, mitigating emotional biases.

- Real-Time Monitoring: The ability to monitor positions in real time allows traders to respond swiftly to market movements. Software equipped with alert systems informs traders of significant events or changes, enabling timely adjustments to safeguard positions or capitalize on opportunities.

- Risk Management: Integral to trade management software is its risk analysis and management features. Traders can assess potential risk exposure across various scenarios, enabling them to adjust their strategies proactively to manage risk effectively.

Selecting the right software for trade management involves a tailored approach, considering individual trading styles, strategies, and objectives. The ideal software suite should offer:

- Customizability: The software must provide a high degree of customization, allowing traders to tailor the platform to their specific trading needs and preferences, particularly for complex strategies like the iron condor.

- Analytical Capabilities: Robust analytical tools, including advanced charting, technical indicators, and backtesting functionalities, are critical for strategy development and refinement.

- Integration with Trading Platforms: Seamless integration with trading platforms ensures that traders can execute trades directly from the software, streamlining the trading process.

- Support for Algorithmic Trading: For traders inclined

towards algorithmic trading, the software should support the development and implementation of trading algorithms, offering a competitive edge in strategy execution.

The evolution of trade management software is marked by the incorporation of cutting-edge technologies such as artificial intelligence (AI) and machine learning. These technologies offer predictive insights into market movements, enhance risk assessment models, and automate routine trading tasks, thereby elevating the strategic positioning of traders.

- AI-Powered Analytics: AI algorithms analyze vast datasets to uncover market trends and patterns, offering traders predictive insights that inform better decision-making.

- Machine Learning for Strategy Optimization: Machine learning models adapt and refine trading strategies based on historical data and evolving market conditions, optimizing the performance of strategies like the iron condor over time.

The meticulous selection and utilization of trade management software stand at the core of modern trading strategies, particularly for those engaging with complex options strategies like the iron condor. By harnessing the power of advanced software solutions, traders can navigate the market with greater confidence, efficiency, and strategic acumen. As we continue to witness technological advancements in trade management software, traders who adeptly integrate these tools into their trading practices are poised to achieve sustained success in the dynamic world of options trading.

The Role of Automation and Bots in Streamlining Iron Condor Trades

Automation in trade management is the principle of minimizing human error while maximizing operational efficiency. Automation in the context of iron condor trading involves the use of software to execute predefined trading strategies without the need for continuous manual intervention. This enables traders to:

- Execute Timely Trades: Automation ensures that trades are executed at the optimal moment, based on predefined criteria, thereby capitalizing on market opportunities as they arise.

- Maintain Discipline: By removing emotional decision-making from the equation, automation helps maintain trading discipline, ensuring that the trading plan is followed meticulously.

- Scale Operations: With automation, traders can manage a larger volume of iron condor positions simultaneously, scaling their trading operations beyond what would be feasible manually.

Algorithmic bots elevate the concept of automation by introducing complex algorithms into the decision-making process. These bots analyze market data, predict trends, and make decisions on executing or adjusting iron condor positions in real-time, based on sophisticated mathematical models. The capabilities of algorithmic bots include:

- Market Analysis: Leveraging vast amounts of market data to predict future movements with a high degree of accuracy, enabling proactive strategy adjustments.

- Risk Management: Automatically adjusting positions to manage risk exposure, based on real-time market conditions and predefined risk parameters.

- Strategy Optimization: Continuously learning from market conditions and past performance to optimize trading strategies for improved outcomes.

The integration of bots in iron condor trading requires a careful approach to ensure alignment with the trader's objectives and risk tolerance. Key considerations include:

- Customization: Developing or customizing bots to suit the specific requirements of the iron condor strategy, taking into account variables such as strike prices, expiration dates, and market indicators.

- Backtesting: Rigorously backtesting bots using historical market data to validate their effectiveness and refine their algorithms before deploying them in live trading environments.

- Monitoring: While bots can operate autonomously, continuous monitoring is essential to oversee their performance, intervene in case of anomalies, and make adjustments as market conditions evolve.

The future of automation and bots in iron condor trading is intrinsically linked with advancements in artificial intelligence (AI) and machine learning. As these technologies continue to evolve, we can anticipate an era where bots not only execute trades but also possess cognitive abilities to make complex trading decisions, learn from their successes and failures, and adapt their strategies in real-time to dynamic market conditions.

The advent of automation and algorithmic bots has undeniably transformed the art and science of iron condor trading. By embracing these technological innovations, traders can enhance the precision, efficiency, and profitability of their trading strategies. However, the successful integration of bots into trading practices necessitates a deep understanding of both the technology and the underlying trading strategy. As we forge ahead, the symbiosis of human insight and algorithmic efficiency will undoubtedly shape the future of options trading, making it more accessible, effective, and adaptive to the ever-evolving financial markets.

CHAPTER 9: BUILDING A LONG-TERM IRON CONDOR PORTFOLIO

The cornerstone of a resilient long-term iron condor portfolio lies in diversification. Unlike traditional stock portfolios where diversification typically involves different sectors or asset classes, diversification in an iron condor portfolio encompasses:

- Underlying Assets: Spread positions across a variety of stocks, indices, and ETFs to mitigate sector-specific risks and capitalize on different volatility patterns.

- Expiration Dates: Staggering expiration dates provides a temporal spread, reducing the impact of market events on the entire portfolio at any given time and smoothing out returns.

- Strategic Variations: Employing variations of the iron condor strategy, such as wide or tight spreads, to adapt to changing market conditions and volatility levels.

A static portfolio in the dynamic landscape of options trading is a recipe for stagnation. Adaptability involves:

- Continuous Market Analysis: Staying abreast of market trends, economic indicators, and geopolitical events that could influence market volatility and, consequently, the performance of the iron condors.

- Regular Portfolio Review and Adjustment: Periodically assessing the portfolio's performance, removing underperforming positions, and adjusting strategies in response to new information or market forecasts.

Effective risk management is critical in preserving capital and ensuring the long-term viability of the iron condor portfolio. Key risk management techniques include:

- Position Sizing: Limiting the capital allocated to any single iron condor to a fraction of the total portfolio to prevent significant losses from any single trade.

- Stop-Loss Orders: Setting stop-loss orders for positions that move against the forecast to cap potential losses.

- Hedging: Utilizing protective options strategies as a hedge against unforeseen market movements that could adversely affect open iron condor positions.

While leveraging can amplify profits, its use within an iron condor portfolio must be approached with caution due to the increased risk of significant losses. If employed, leverage should be:

- Calculated and Conservative: Restricted to a small portion of the portfolio and based on rigorous analysis to justify the increased risk.

- Monitored Closely: Leveraged positions require constant monitoring to quickly respond to unfavorable market movements.

In today's trading environment, technology plays a pivotal role in managing a long-term iron condor portfolio. Automated trading platforms, risk analysis software, and real-time market data feeds are invaluable tools in:

- Executing Trades: Automating trade execution based on predefined criteria to capitalize on market opportunities swiftly.

- Monitoring Positions: Utilizing software to monitor open positions in real-time, providing alerts on critical events or indicators that necessitate action.

- Analyzing Performance: Employing analytics tools to evaluate the portfolio's performance, identify strengths and weaknesses, and refine strategies accordingly.

The final piece in building a long-term iron condor portfolio is the trader's commitment to continuous education and community engagement. Participating in forums, attending workshops, and networking with fellow traders enrich a trader's knowledge base, providing new insights and strategies to incorporate into the portfolio.

Building and managing a long-term iron condor portfolio is an endeavor that marries the analytical precision of strategy with the art of adaptation and risk management. It demands not only a thorough understanding of the options market but also the patience to let strategies unfold and the agility to adjust as market conditions change. For those who master it, the long-term iron condor portfolio stands as a beacon of financial acumen, offering both stability and profitability in the ever-changing tapestry of the options trading world.

Diversifying Your Iron Condor Positions

Iron condors, by their nature, capitalize on market stability. However, relying on a single market or asset for premium income risks exposure to unforeseen events. Thus, the first step towards diversification is the selection of varied underlyings. Equity indexes, for instance, offer a broad market exposure, mitigating risks associated with individual stocks. Yet, venturing into commodities or currency-based ETFs can introduce a new dimension of volatility and opportunity, broadening the spectrum of risk and reward. Diversification across sectors - technology, healthcare, industrials - further hedges against sector-specific downturns, allowing traders to capture premiums across a variety of economic landscapes.

Time, an often overlooked dimension, plays a critical role in the crafting of iron condor strategies. Diversifying across different expiration periods can significantly affect the risk profile of an iron condor portfolio. Short-term contracts, while offering quicker returns, require closer monitoring and potentially higher adjustment frequencies. Conversely, longer-term iron condors, though possibly less sensitive to immediate market movements, demand a patience and commitment to longer periods of capital tie-up. A strategic blend of varying expirations not only spreads risk over time but also allows traders to capitalize on different market sentiments and volatility environments.

Not all iron condors are crafted alike; nuances in strike selection, width of spreads, and risk-to-reward ratios offer a playground for diversification. A tighter condor, seeking to maximize premium on low-volatility stocks, contrasts sharply with a wider condor that, while accepting lower premiums, provides a greater buffer against market movements. Additionally, adjusting the proportion of bullish versus bearish iron condors in response to market cycles—leaning into bullish spreads in rising markets and favoring bearish spreads in downturns—can add a dynamic layer of strategic diversification.

The crux of diversifying iron condor positions lies in meticulous portfolio management. Balancing different underlyings, time frames, and strategies requires a continuous assessment of market conditions and portfolio performance. Utilizing tools such as beta weighting and delta-neutral adjustments assists in maintaining a balanced exposure, minimizing systemic risks, and aligning the portfolio with the trader's risk tolerance and market outlook.

In diversifying, one must be wary of systemic risks that transcend individual securities or sectors. Economic downturns, geopolitical events, or significant policy changes can induce correlations among seemingly diverse underlyings, potentially undermining diversification efforts. Regularly reviewing the correlation matrix of your positions and staying attuned to macroeconomic indicators can provide early warnings, allowing for preemptive adjustments to the portfolio.

The fabric of the iron condor strategy is woven with threads of risk management, strategic foresight, and, crucially, diversification. Diversification across different underlyings isn't merely a tactic but a cornerstone philosophy that underpins the resilience and performance of an iron condor portfolio. Venturing into this realm necessitates a keen eye for detail, an understanding of varying market behaviors, and the ability to synergize these elements into a cohesive strategy. This explorative journey into diversification illuminates the nuanced approach required to navigate the complexities of multiple underlyings.

Underlying assets in an iron condor strategy act as the foundation upon which the positions are built. These assets can range from individual stocks and ETFs to broad market indexes. Each category of underlying brings with it a unique set of characteristics—volatility patterns, sectoral influences, and correlation with wider market movements. The choice of underlyings is a delicate balance between seeking diversity to mitigate risks and aligning with the trader's insight into future market directions.

Equity indexes, such as the S&P 500 or the NASDAQ-100, are popular choices for their broad market representation. They offer a natural hedge against the idiosyncratic risks present in individual stocks. By incorporating these indexes into an iron condor portfolio, a trader can capitalize on general market stability or mild fluctuations, which are the ideal conditions for iron condor profitability.

Sector-specific ETFs provide a targeted approach to diversification. By analyzing economic cycles, traders can position their iron condors in sectors poised for relative stability or predictable movement. For instance, during periods of economic recovery, cyclical sectors like consumer discretionary might offer favorable conditions for iron condors, given their potential for steady growth without extreme volatility.

The inclusion of ETFs tracking international markets or specific countries introduces a geographical dimension to diversification. These underlyings can be pivotal in spreading risk during times when the U.S. market faces turbulence, as global markets might not mirror the U.S. market's movements precisely. However, this strategy demands a comprehensive understanding of global economic indicators, foreign policy impacts, and currency risks.

Commodities and currency-based ETFs or futures offer an advanced layer of diversification. These assets often exhibit low correlation with stock markets and can serve as a hedge against inflation or currency devaluation. Incorporating commodities like gold or oil into an iron condor strategy could safeguard a portfolio against market-wide shocks, albeit at the cost of higher complexity and monitoring requirements.

The process of selecting underlyings for an iron condor portfolio is akin to assembling a mosaic—each piece must fit perfectly within the broader picture. This task involves continuous research, backtesting, and scenario analysis to understand how different underlyings respond to market conditions. Diversification is not a 'set and forget' strategy; it requires ongoing adjustment and rebalancing to align with evolving market dynamics and personal risk tolerance.

While diversification across underlyings can significantly mitigate risk, it does not eliminate it. Each additional underlying introduces complexity and requires independent monitoring. The key is to find a balance where the benefits of diversification outweigh the costs of complexity. Effective use of risk management tools and techniques, such as stop-loss orders and portfolio beta adjustments, becomes indispensable in this multifaceted trading environment.

diversifying across different underlyings in an iron condor strategy presents a methodical approach to enhancing portfolio resilience. It navigates the fine line between risk and reward, employing depth and breadth of market exposure to create a bulwark against uncertainty. This strategic component underscores the essence of sophisticated trading—turning insight into action and challenges into opportunities.

Across Time Frames

Iron condor trading, by its nature, is a play on market stability and time decay. The selection of time frames for opening positions is pivotal, as it influences both the risk profile and potential returns of the strategy. Short, medium, and long-term time frames each come with their distinct characteristics and implications for an iron condor strategy, forming a temporal tapestry that traders must weave with precision and insight.

Short-term iron condor positions, typically spanning weeks to a month, offer traders the advantage of agility. These positions are highly responsive to immediate market conditions, allowing traders to capitalize on short-term stability or mild fluctuations. However, the rapid time decay inherent in these positions demands vigilance and a proactive stance on risk management. The success of short-term trades hinges on precise timing and the ability to quickly adapt to market movements.

Medium-term positions, extending from one to several months, strike a balance between the immediacy of short-term trades and the patience required for long-term positions. This time frame allows for a more measured response to market developments, providing a buffer against the volatility that can plague shorter-term trades. The medium-term horizon is particularly conducive to capturing seasonality effects and cyclical trends, offering traders a blend of stability and flexibility.

Long-term iron condor positions, with durations spanning several months to a year, embody the principle of patience. These trades benefit from a broader perspective, allowing traders to weather short-term market turbulence with an eye on longer-term stability. The extended time frame affords a higher degree of premium collection due to the longer exposure, but it also requires a commitment to thorough research and forward-looking market analysis. Long-term positions are a testament to the trader's confidence in their market outlook and risk management prowess.

Successful iron condor trading across time frames necessitates an attuned sense of market cycles and economic indicators. Traders must synchronize their selection of time frames with their analysis of market phases—expansion, peak, contraction, and trough—to align their strategies with anticipated market conditions. This synchronization enables the deliberate positioning of iron condors to exploit expected periods of stability or mild fluctuations, regardless of the market's broader trajectory.

The essence of diversifying across time frames lies in creating a dynamic equilibrium within the portfolio. This equilibrium balances the immediacy of short-term trades with the foresight of long-term positions, optimizing the portfolio's risk-reward ratio. Temporal diversification requires continuous adjustment, as traders must recalibrate their strategies in response to changing market conditions and shifts in their investment horizons.

diversifying iron condor trades across different time frames introduces a dimension of strategic depth that complements underlying diversification. It embodies a holistic approach to portfolio construction, where time itself becomes an asset to be strategically deployed. Through the meticulous alignment of trades with time frames that resonate with market cycles and personal investment goals, traders can navigate the complexities of options trading with confidence, turning the continuum of time into a canvas for financial success.

With Varying Strategies

The strategic spectrum of iron condor trading spans a wide array of tactics, each tailored to different market sentiments and volatility levels. At one end of the spectrum lies the conservative approach, designed for markets exhibiting low volatility and minimal directional movement. Here, the focus is on safety and steady returns, with wider strike spreads and far-out expiration dates providing a buffer against market swings.

Contrastingly, the aggressive strategy occupies the other end of the spectrum, suited for traders willing to embrace higher risk for potentially greater rewards. This approach thrives in markets characterized by high volatility, employing narrower strike spreads and shorter expiration times to capitalize on significant market movements.

The key to a successful iron condor portfolio lies not in the rigid adherence to a single strategy but in the fluid blending of multiple strategies. This dynamic approach allows traders to adapt to changing market conditions, shifting between conservative and aggressive tactics as the market ebbs and flows. By diversifying strategies within the portfolio, traders can mitigate risks and exploit opportunities across different market environments.

Case Studies: Strategy in Action

To illustrate the practical application of varying strategies, consider the case of a trader who allocates a portion of their portfolio to conservative iron condors during a period of low market volatility. Simultaneously, the trader employs aggressive iron condors in anticipation of an upcoming earnings announcement, poised to capture the heightened volatility. This dual-strategy approach enables the trader to maintain a steady income stream while seizing opportunistic gains, exemplifying the strategic agility essential to iron condor trading.

Tactical Adjustments: Fine-Tuning for Optimal Performance

A crucial component of employing varying strategies is the ability to make tactical adjustments in response to market feedback. This involves closely monitoring open positions and being prepared to adjust strike prices, expiration dates, or even the ratio of conservative to aggressive strategies within the portfolio. For instance, a sudden increase in volatility may prompt a shift towards more conservative positions to preserve capital, while an unexpected market stabilization could signal an opportunity to adopt more aggressive tactics.

Integrating varying strategies into an iron condor portfolio is akin to cultivating a diverse ecosystem, where each strategy plays a distinct role in achieving overall balance and resilience. This strategic ecosystem is continually evolving, guided by the trader's insights and the market's whims. It demands a proactive stance, a keen market sense, and a willingness to adapt strategies in pursuit of optimal performance.

Managing a Large Portfolio

The cornerstone of effective portfolio management lies in its construction. A well-structured portfolio is diversified not only across different underlying assets but also across strategies, expiration dates, and strike prices. This diversification serves as a safeguard against market volatility, reducing the risk inherent in options trading.

A critical aspect of portfolio construction is the selection of underlying assets. These should include a mix of indices, stocks, and ETFs, each chosen for their liquidity, volatility characteristics, and the trader's familiarity with their market behaviors. This selection process underpins the portfolio's potential for success, grounding it in a well-researched foundation.

Dynamic Portfolio Adjustment: Staying Agile

As markets are in constant flux, maintaining an optimal portfolio necessitates ongoing adjustments. These adjustments are twofold: reactive and proactive. Reactive adjustments respond to unforeseen market movements, aiming to mitigate risk and protect gains. Proactive adjustments, on the other hand, are strategic shifts anticipating future market conditions, seizing opportunities for enhanced returns.

A pivotal part of dynamic portfolio management is the use of risk management tools and metrics, such as delta, gamma, and theta. These 'Greeks' provide insights into the portfolio's sensitivity to various market factors, guiding the adjustment process. For instance, a portfolio with a high positive delta may require hedging strategies to balance out the directional risk in a bullish market scenario.

In managing large portfolios, technology plays a crucial role. Advanced trading platforms and analytical tools offer real-time data and insights, enabling traders to make informed decisions swiftly. Automation, particularly in the form of trading bots, can be employed to execute certain adjustments, ensuring timely responses to market triggers.

However, while technology can augment efficiency, it cannot replace the nuanced judgment of an experienced trader. The use of automation should be balanced with hands-on management, ensuring that strategic decisions are underpinned by human insight and experience.

Psychological Resilience: The Trader's Mindset

Beyond the technical and strategic facets, managing a large portfolio demands psychological resilience. The emotional rollercoaster of trading—marked by wins and losses—can be magnified in a large portfolio. Cultivating a disciplined mindset, grounded in a well-considered trading plan and risk management strategy, is essential. This discipline helps in maintaining a long-term perspective, preventing rash decisions driven by short-term market fluctuations.

To concretize these concepts, consider the case of a trader managing a diverse iron condor portfolio through the tumultuous markets of early 2020. As volatility spiked, the trader employed dynamic adjustments, strategically rolling out positions to mitigate risk and capture emerging opportunities. This proactive management—coupled with the disciplined use of stop losses and the judicious application of hedging strategies —underscored the importance of agility and resilience in portfolio management.

Adjusting for Systematic Risk

Systematic risk, or market risk, is the potential for a portfolio's value to decrease due to factors that affect the entire market or asset class. Unlike unsystematic risk, which can be diversified away by holding a variety of assets, systematic risk is inescapable through diversification alone. It encompasses economic recessions, political turmoil, changes in interest rates, and natural disasters—forces that impact the market in its entirety.

The cornerstone of combating systematic risk lies in effective hedging strategies. Hedging involves taking a position in a security or derivative that will gain as your main portfolio loses, offsetting potential losses. For iron condor traders, this might include:

- Index Options: Utilizing index options as a hedge can protect against broad market movements. If a trader's portfolio is primarily bullish, purchasing put options on a major market index can provide insurance against market downturns.

- Inverse ETFs: These are exchange-traded funds designed to perform as the inverse of an index or benchmark. Holding inverse ETFs as part of the portfolio can act as a counterbalance during market declines.

Utilizing Beta for Portfolio Calibration

Beta, a measure of a security's volatility relative to the overall market, plays a pivotal role in adjusting for systematic risk. A portfolio with a high beta is more vulnerable to market fluctuations. By carefully selecting assets with lower or negative betas, traders can reduce the portfolio's overall sensitivity to market movements.

For iron condor portfolios, assessing the beta of underlying assets and adjusting positions accordingly can help in managing exposure to systematic risk. This might involve skewing the portfolio towards assets with a beta closer to zero during times of anticipated market volatility.

While traditional diversification—spreading investments across various sectors or asset classes—has limited effectiveness against systematic risk, diversification across strategies and time horizons can offer additional layers of protection. For instance, mixing iron condors with strategies that thrive in volatile markets, such as straddles or strangles, can provide a hedge against broad market movements.

Additionally, diversifying expiry dates and strike prices within the iron condor strategy itself can help manage exposure to systematic events. By not having all positions expire or react within the same timeframe, traders can avoid the pitfalls of a synchronized negative response to market changes.

Systematic Risk and the Macro View

Understanding and adjusting for systematic risk requires a keen eye on macroeconomic indicators and market sentiment. Traders need to stay informed about global economic trends, interest rate decisions, and geopolitical events. This macro view, combined with the strategies outlined above, enables traders to navigate the unpredictable seas of market-wide risks.

In Practice: A Thematic Approach to Systematic Risk

Consider the hypothetical scenario of an iron condor trader in the lead-up to a significant election. Anticipating increased market volatility, the trader employs a mix of hedging strategies, including purchasing index puts and adjusting the beta exposure of their portfolio. By also diversifying their expiries and employing straddles on select positions, they create a robust framework capable of withstanding the shockwaves of the election results.

While systematic risk presents a formidable challenge, it is not insurmountable. Through a combination of strategic hedging, careful beta management, and diversified strategy application, traders can construct iron condor portfolios that stand resilient in the face of market-wide disturbances. This proactive approach not only safeguards investments but also empowers traders to pursue opportunities with confidence, regardless of the market's vicissitudes.

Correlation and Portfolio Risk Management

Correlation, in the financial vernacular, refers to the statistical measure that quantifies the extent to which two securities move in relation to each other. Correlation coefficients range from -1 to 1. A correlation of 1 implies that the two assets move in perfect unison, a correlation of -1 denotes they move in exact opposite directions, and a correlation of 0 indicates no relationship in the movement patterns of the assets.

For iron condor traders, understanding and applying correlation is crucial for two reasons. Firstly, it aids in identifying underlying assets that, when combined in a portfolio, reduce vulnerability to market volatilities. Secondly, it helps in pinpointing assets that, due to their inverse relationship, offer a natural hedge against each other.

Strategic Application of Correlation in Portfolio Construction

The art of portfolio construction with an eye on correlation involves a judicious selection of assets that exhibit low or negative correlation with each other. The objective is to create a portfolio where, if one part is exposed to adverse movements, the impact is mitigated or offset by the performance of the other components.

For instance, in an environment where technology stocks are highly correlated and expected to experience volatility, an iron condor trader might balance the portfolio with positions in utilities or consumer staples, sectors often exhibiting lower correlation with tech stocks. This strategic diversification ensures that not all portfolio components are impacted simultaneously by the same market event.

Market conditions are fluid, and the correlation between assets can shift in response to economic indicators, geopolitical events, and changes in market sentiment. A critical skill for traders is the ability to dynamically adjust their portfolios in anticipation of or in response to these shifts in correlation.

This might involve regularly conducting correlation analysis using historical price data and adjusting the portfolio composition to ensure alignment with the desired risk management strategy. In doing so, traders can preemptively rebalance their portfolios, reducing exposure to anticipated market shifts.

Correlation and Iron Condor Strategy Optimization

In optimizing iron condor strategies, correlation analysis extends beyond the selection of underlying assets. It also pertains to the alignment of strike prices and expiration dates across these assets. By intelligently managing these parameters in correlation with market movements and sentiments, traders can fine-tune their iron condor positions for optimal balance between risk and reward.

For example, during periods of expected low market volatility, a trader might deploy iron condors on assets that are historically negatively correlated. This approach can potentially amplify returns by capitalizing on the minimal market movements. Conversely, in high volatility periods, selecting assets with low intra-correlation for iron condor positions can help in mitigating risk.

Practical Insights: Correlation in Action

Consider a practical scenario where an iron condor trader monitors the correlation between the S&P 500 index and a basket of pharmaceutical companies. Observing a decreasing correlation amidst regulatory changes affecting the healthcare sector, the trader decides to adjust the portfolio by increasing positions in the pharmaceutical sector while reducing exposure to the S&P 500 index options. This strategic maneuver aims to leverage the diverging paths of these assets to stabilize the portfolio against broader market swings.

Correlation, when skillfully applied, becomes an indispensable tool in the construction of a well-tuned iron condor portfolio. It empowers traders to navigate the complexities of market interrelations with a strategy that not only mitigates risk but also positions the portfolio to capitalize on diverse market dynamics. As traders evolve in their mastery of correlation analysis, they unlock new dimensions of strategic portfolio management, enabling them to remain agile and resilient in the ever-changing tapestry of the financial markets.

The Importance of Cash Reserves

The rationale for holding cash reserves in an iron condor trading strategy is multifaceted, serving not just as a bulwark against unforeseen market downturns but also as a springboard for capitalizing on emergent opportunities. In turbulent markets, cash reserves act as a shock absorber, dampening the impact of adverse price movements on the overall portfolio. This liquidity buffer ensures that traders are not forced into untimely liquidation of positions at unfavorable prices, thereby preserving the integrity of the trading strategy and the trader's capital.

Furthermore, cash reserves are instrumental in maintaining flexibility within the portfolio. In moments when the market presents unanticipated opportunities, be it through mispriced options or sudden shifts in volatility, having immediate access to liquidity allows traders to swiftly pivot and seize these opportunities, potentially enhancing the portfolio's performance.

Quantifying the Optimal Level of Cash Reserves

Determining the optimal size of cash reserves is a balancing act, intricately tied to the trader's risk tolerance, trading strategy, and market outlook. While too little cash might leave the portfolio exposed to liquidity crises, an excessive cash position could dampen overall portfolio returns, given that cash, in itself, is a non-yielding asset.

A pragmatic approach involves assessing the portfolio's exposure to market volatilities and the frequency and scale of trading opportunities historically capitalized on. This assessment, combined with a thorough understanding of the trader's risk appetite, guides the calibration of cash reserves to an optimal level that mitigates risk without significantly diluting returns.

In the specific context of iron condor trading, cash reserves serve multiple strategic purposes. They provide the flexibility to adjust positions in response to market movements, such as rolling out options to future expirations, widening the strikes of existing positions, or even closing out positions to mitigate losses. Additionally, cash reserves enable the trader to scale up the strategy by increasing the number of iron condor positions held during periods of favorable market conditions, thus amplifying the potential for returns.

Case Study: The Strategic Allocation of Cash Reserves

Consider the scenario of an iron condor trader who meticulously maintains a 20% cash reserve in their portfolio. Amidst a sudden spike in market volatility, many options traders find themselves in a liquidity crunch, forced to close positions at a loss. Our trader, cushioned by the cash reserves, not only avoids such forced closures but also identifies and exploits mispriced options, expanding the portfolio's exposure to iron condors at attractive premiums. This strategic deployment of cash reserves not only protects the portfolio but also positions it for enhanced returns once market volatility subsides.

Cash Reserves, the Unsung Hero of Iron Condor Trading

In the nuanced strategy of iron condor trading, cash reserves hold a place of paramount importance, not as idle capital but as a dynamic tool for risk management and strategic agility. The art of optimizing cash reserves is akin to mastering an instrument in the symphony of trading strategies, where the right balance amplifies the harmony of returns and risk mitigation. As traders advance in their journey, the thoughtful allocation of cash reserves becomes a testament to their strategic acumen, empowering them to navigate the markets with confidence and resilience.

Advanced Strategies for Sustained Success

One of the cornerstones of sustained success in iron condor trading is the ability to dynamically adjust positions in response to market movements. This involves a granular understanding of the Greeks (Delta, Gamma, Theta, and Vega) and how they affect the performance of an iron condor. For instance, a seasoned trader monitors the Delta of their positions closely, ready to make adjustments when the market moves against their predictions. This might involve rolling the affected side of the condor to a different strike price or expiration date, effectively managing the risk and preserving the potential for profit.

While iron condors represent a neutral strategy ideal for range-bound markets, diversification remains a pivotal strategy for sustained success. Experienced practitioners of the iron condor often diversify their portfolios not just across different underlying assets but also through incorporating complementary strategies. For example, integrating vertical spreads or straddles alongside iron condors can provide additional profit avenues during unexpected market volatility. This strategic diversification ensures that the trader's portfolio is well-positioned to capitalize on various market conditions.

In today's digital age, the astute use of technology and software is a game-changer for iron condor traders. Advanced trading platforms equipped with analytical tools enable traders to simulate various scenarios and identify the most promising strategies before execution. Furthermore, algorithmic trading bots can be programmed to automatically execute trades based on specific criteria, such as changes in volatility or price movements, ensuring that opportunities are never missed. Leveraging these technological advancements allows traders to stay a step ahead in the market.

A often overlooked aspect of trading success is the psychological resilience required to navigate the highs and lows of the market. The seasoned iron condor trader cultivates a mindset of detachment from individual trades, focusing instead on the long-term performance of their portfolio. This psychological fortitude is complemented by a commitment to continuous education. Markets evolve, and strategies that were effective yesterday may not suffice tomorrow. Hence, the successful trader is always learning, whether through reading the latest financial literature, attending workshops, or engaging with a community of fellow traders.

Case Study: The Evolution of a Trading Strategy

Consider the journey of Alex, an experienced trader who has been deploying iron condor strategies for a decade. Alex's early success was marked by the rigorous application of standard iron condor setups. However, as market conditions shifted, Alex noticed a gradual erosion in profitability. Undeterred, Alex embarked on a quest for education, diving into advanced options trading literature and experimenting with dynamic adjustment strategies. By integrating technology for real-time analytics and adopting a diversified approach to trading strategies, Alex not only recovered the portfolio's performance but also set it on a path of sustained success.

Achieving sustained success in iron condor trading is akin to mastering a complex craft. It requires an amalgamation of strategic foresight, psychological resilience, technological savvy, and an unyielding commitment to learning. The advanced strategies outlined herein are not mere tactics but principles that guide the trader towards a deeper understanding of the markets and themselves. As traders refine their approach and adapt to the ever-changing financial landscapes, they unlock the potential for not just survival but prosperity in the world of options trading.

Continuous Learning and Education

a successful iron condor trader's philosophy is the unwavering commitment to lifelong learning. The financial markets are not static entities—they are vibrant ecosystems that reflect the pulse of the global economy, technological advancements, and geopolitical shifts. As such, traders must adopt a proactive approach to education, seeking out new knowledge, challenging their own understandings, and being open to the evolution of their strategies.

A structured approach to learning can significantly enhance a trader's ability to comprehend complex concepts and apply them effectively. This includes formal education such as courses in financial analysis, options trading, and risk management, offered by accredited institutions and online platforms. Furthermore, certification programs and specialized workshops provide focused learning opportunities on advanced trading strategies and analytical tools.

Simulation platforms represent a critical tool in the trader's educational arsenal, allowing for the application of theoretical knowledge in a risk-free environment. Through simulated trading experiences, individuals can experiment with various iron condor setups, test different adjustment strategies in response to simulated market movements, and refine their decision-making process without the immediate pressure of real-world consequences. This hands-on approach facilitates deeper learning and accelerates the development of expertise.

Mentorship and community engagement offer unparalleled value in continuous education. By connecting with experienced traders and mentors, individuals can gain insights into the practical nuances of trading that are often not covered in textbooks. Online forums, trading clubs, and seminars provide platforms for knowledge exchange, discussion, and debate, fostering a communal learning environment that enriches individual experience.

IRON CONDOR TRADING SCENARIOS

1. Earnings Announcement

- **Objective**: Capitalize on volatility crush post-announcement.

- **Execution**: Establish the iron condor just before the earnings release when implied volatility (IV) is high. Choose expiration dates that are shortly after the earnings announcement to maximize the impact of the volatility crush.

2. Range-Bound Market

- **Objective**: Profit from a lack of movement.

- **Execution**: Identify the range within which the market or stock has been trading. Set your strikes for the call and put spreads just outside of this range, betting that the price will stay within these bounds.

3. High Volatility Environment

- **Objective**: Take advantage of decreasing volatility.

- **Execution**: After a period of high volatility, look for signs of stabilization. Place the iron condor with the expectation that the asset will not make a significant move and that IV will decrease.

4. Pre-Fed Announcements

- **Objective**: Profit from a volatility drop post-announcement.

- **Execution**: Place the trade a few days before the Fed announcement when IV might be higher. Choose an expiration shortly after the announcement to exploit the potential volatility drop.

5. Sector Rotation

- **Objective**: Profit from a cooling off sector.

- **Execution**: Identify the ETF that represents the cooling sector. Set up the iron condor with strikes that reflect the expected consolidation range.

6. Political Events

- **Objective**: Capitalize on uncertainty reduction post-event.

- **Execution**: Similar to the earnings announcement strategy, place the iron condor before the event when IV is elevated, betting on a volatility crush once the outcome is known.

7. Currency Stability

- **Objective**: Profit from stable exchange rates.

- **Execution**: After significant fluctuations, set the iron condor on the currency pair expected to stabilize, with strikes outside the expected stability range.

8. After a Big Move

- **Objective**: Profit from market consolidation.

- **Execution**: After a significant move, wait for signs of consolidation. Place your iron condor with the expectation that the asset will remain within a certain range during this period.

9. Interest Rate Decisions

- **Objective**: Take advantage of market non-reaction.

- **Execution**: If the decision is expected to be a non-event, place the iron condor just before, using the market's current range to guide your strike selection, betting on stability.

10. Commodity Stabilization

- **Objective**: Profit from commodity price stabilization.

- **Execution**: After significant moves due to supply and demand factors, place the iron condor on futures or ETFs, predicting the commodity will remain within a defined range.

General Tips for Execution:

- **Choosing Strikes**: The sold call and put should be out of the money, reflecting your prediction of the price staying within a range. The bought options act as insurance, limiting potential losses.

- **Risk Management**: Always be aware of the maximum potential loss, which occurs if the price of the underlying asset moves beyond either the highest or lowest strike prices.

- **Adjustments**: If the market moves against your position, consider adjusting the trade by rolling the threatened side (calls or puts) to further out strikes or closing the position early to manage losses.

- **Expiration**: Choosing the right expiration is crucial. Shorter-term options will be more sensitive to IV changes, which can be advantageous in scenarios expecting a volatility drop.

Executing an iron condor requires careful planning and consideration of market conditions, expected events, and individual risk tolerance. It's also important to monitor these trades, as market conditions can change, necessitating adjustments to the original positions.

ADDITIONAL RESOURCES

Books

1. "Options as a Strategic Investment" by Lawrence G. McMillan - This comprehensive guide offers deep insights into options trading, serving as an essential resource for both beginners and seasoned professionals looking to expand their knowledge base.

2. "Trading Options Greeks: How Time, Volatility, and Other Pricing Factors Drive Profits" by Dan Passarelli - Focuses on how different Greeks can be used to analyze and improve trading strategies.

3. "The Options Playbook" by Brian Overby - Provides a straightforward, easy-to-understand explanation of various options trading strategies, including the iron condor.

4. "Volatility Trading" by Euan Sinclair - Offers insight into how volatility can be a critical aspect of options trading.

5. "Option Volatility & Pricing: Advanced Trading Strategies and Techniques" by Sheldon Natenberg - A staple for any options trader, this book dives deep into volatility and pricing models.

Articles and Online Resources

1. Investopedia - Features numerous articles on options trading, including strategies, terminologies, and practical examples.

2. The Options Industry Council (OIC) - Provides free educational materials, webinars, and tools for options traders at all levels.

3. Seeking Alpha - Offers insightful articles and analysis on options strategies from various contributors.

4. CBOE (Chicago Board Options Exchange) Education - Offers comprehensive resources, including online learning tools, seminars, and webcasts for options traders.

5. Tastytrade - An online network that provides real trading examples and educational shows focused on options trading.

Organizations

1. Options Clearing Corporation (OCC) - Provides central counterparty clearing and settlement services to the options markets.

2. Professional Risk Managers' International Association (PRMIA) - Offers educational resources, certification programs, and networking opportunities for risk management professionals.

Tools and Software

1. OptionNET Explorer - A comprehensive software solution that provides simulation and analysis tools for evaluating options trading strategies.

2. thinkorswim by TD Ameritrade - An advanced trading platform that offers powerful trading tools, including options strategy scanners and analysis tools.

3. Interactive Brokers - Offers a robust trading platform with extensive options trading capabilities, including risk management tools and simulations.

4. Option Samurai - Provides an easy-to-use platform for scanning for options strategies, including the iron condor, based on specified criteria.

5. TradeStation - A trading platform that caters to options traders with its advanced analysis tools and customizable charts for strategy evaluation.

Conclusion

This collection of resources serves as a comprehensive supplement to "Iron Condor Decoded: Strategic Earnings through Options," catering to professionals eager to refine their options trading strategies through enhanced theoretical understanding and the application of sophisticated techniques. Whether through in-depth books, informative articles, interactive tools, supportive organizations, or advanced software, these resources offer valuable avenues for both learning and practical application in options trading.

Made in the USA
Las Vegas, NV
08 February 2025